THE COUNTRY GENTLEMAN

The Untold Story of

"ALLEN KARL" STERNER

THE
COUNTRY
GENTLEMAN

The Untold Story of
"ALLEN KARL" STERNER

JULIE RICHARDSON

FOREWORD *by*

GLENN R. SCHIRALDI, PH.D.

Golden Country, LLC

The Country Gentleman
The Untold Story of "Allen Karl" Sterner

Golden Country, LLC

For information write:
Golden Country, LLC PO Box 1111 Lenoir, North Carolina 28645

Publisher: Golden Country, LLC
Front Cover Photo Credit: Courtesy of the Sterner family & Rafel Corbi
Back Cover Photo Credit: Matthew Coates
Author Photo: Brindi Low
All Photos Courtesy of the Sterner family unless otherwise noted.

Editors: Earlene Smith & Julie Richardson
Interior Layout Design: Nick Zelinger

ISBN 978-0-578-32754-9 (hard cover)

Library of Congress Control Number: 2022944846

First Edition

Printed in the United States of America

Acknowledgments

I want to extend a special thank you to Allen Karl for his trust and faith in me to write his life story. I appreciate the countless hours you've given to me in personal interviews, photo shoots, and tours of your old stomping grounds. You've stayed with me every step of the way and I can't thank you enough for your patience and support as I worked through the process of writing this book.

A nod of tremendous gratitude to Jerry Sterner for his willingness to share his experiences and insights for this book. I know you endured your own suffering and want you to know that I admire you for the man you are today.

Thank you to the entire Sterner family for providing me with pictures, personal interviews, stories, articles, and support throughout my writing process. Janelle, thank you especially for your enthusiasm, hospitality, and vote of confidence in me to write your father's story.

Dr. Glenn Schiraldi, I am grateful for your words, wisdom, and willingness to write the foreword for Allen's book. I know we both greatly admire you and feel truly blessed that you are part of this inspiring story.

A heartfelt thank you to Allen's cousin, Professor Geoff Beadle, for his extraordinary talent and for spending his precious time creating the original sketches for this book. You did a beautiful job, and Allen is so grateful to have your artwork framed to proudly display and treasure for years to come.

I want to thank handwriting analysis experts, Brenda Petty and Marty Pearce for graciously donating their time and expertise to this project. Your input on the letter sent to Pop was priceless and answered some especially important questions for Allen.

Allen would like to extend his gratitude to A.V. Tidmore who was instrumental in giving him his break in music at the age of fourteen.

To Harvey, thank you for looking after Allen as he faced some of the darkest and most difficult battles of his life. Without your warm presence, love, and guidance, Allen wouldn't have made it.

To my mom Carley, as always, I appreciate your love and support in everything I do. With all my love and admiration.

Dedicated to my Sicilian grandfather, Pop.
Without your guidance and help throughout my childhood
I could not have survived for even one minute and would not
be the man that I am today. Pop, I am forever grateful to you
and will always love you with all my heart. –Allen

Contents

Foreword

"While reading, we don't fall in love with the character's appearance,
we fall in love with their words, their thoughts, and their hearts.
Ultimately, we fall in love with their souls."
–Unknown

How is it that some people can wade through hell and yet become caring, capable, and fruitful individuals?

Allen Karl is an extraordinary man. The unspeakable cruelty and chaos in his childhood has given him every reason to turn to bitterness, drugs, suicide, and violence. Many who experience less adversity in childhood than he, become mentally or physically ill and functionally impaired. Instead, Allen became a beloved father who never struck his children. He succeeded in marriage, military service, business, and the music industry. Those who know him love him, because he tries to give others a leg up, treating them with respect and kindness.

No one is perfect. This book doesn't claim Allen is. Yet despite his inner wounds, he has strived to learn from his struggles and live an exemplary life-one that elevates others and himself.

I cried many times in reading his story-in sadness for the suffering inflicted on innocent children by troubled adults, and for Allen's burdens in adulthood; in awe for what he has been able to accomplish and the beauty he has given the world; and in joy and admiration for his inner triumphs.

This is a story of the magnificent resilience of the human spirit. In interviewing combat survivors, Navy SEALs, prisoners of war, and survivors of sexual violence, I see common threads and strengths among successful copers. Allen demonstrates these strengths to an extraordinary degree. You'll discover them in these pages. Yet each individual who triumphs over adversity, as he has, does so in a unique way that uplifts and gives us hope.

This isn't just the story of a celebrity's achievements. It is also the story of a little boy who sought the light and to a great degree found it. Ultimately, Allen's story is one of hope, love, determination, faith, goodness, and inspiration. I feel blessed to know Allen, and I am so grateful for the gift of his story.

Glenn R. Schiraldi, Ph.D., Lt. Colonel (USAR, Ret.)
University of Maryland School of Public Health (Ret.)
Author: *The Adverse Childhood Experiences Recovery Workbook; The Post-Traumatic Stress Disorder Sourcebook; The Resilience Workbook; World War II Survivors: Lessons in Resilience; The Self-Esteem Workbook;* and others.

Glenn R. Schiraldi, Ph.D., Lt. Colonel (USAR, Ret.), has served on the stress management faculties at the Pentagon, the International Critical Incident Stress Foundation, and the University of Maryland School of Public Health, where he received the Outstanding Teaching Award and other teaching/service awards. His fourteen books on stress-related topics have been translated into seventeen foreign languages and include: *The Resilience Workbook; The Post-Traumatic Stress Disorder Sourcebook; The Self-Esteem Workbook;* and *World War II Survivors: Lessons in Resilience.*

His latest book, T*he Adverse Childhood Experiences Recovery Workbook,* helps people heal the hidden wounds from toxic childhood stress, which lead to a wide array of adult medical and psychological disorders.

Dr. Schiraldi's writing has been recognized by various scholarly and popular sources, such as the *Washington Post, American Journal of Health Promotion, the Mind/Body Health Review,* and the *International Stress and Tension Control Society Newslette*r.

He has trained high-risk groups (such as the military, police, and firefighters), mental health professionals, and laypersons around the world on various aspects of resilience, stress, and trauma.

His research at the University of Maryland has found that resilience skills training increases resilience, happiness, self-esteem, optimism, and curiosity, while reducing anxiety, depression, and anger.

He is the founder of Resilience Training International (www.ResilienceFirst.com), which teaches people how to prevent and recover from stress-related conditions (such as PTSD, depression, and anxiety), while optimizing mental health and performance under pressure. He and his wife led an addiction recovery group for years.

Glenn is a graduate of the U.S. Military Academy, West Point, and a Vietnam-era veteran. His doctorate is from University of Maryland.

Introduction

"I Am Fine, Thank You."

*"One day you will tell your story about how you overcame what
you went through, and it'll be someone else's survival guide."*
–Brene Brown

Mesmerized by the glowing, flickering flame of a comforting fire contained within a large, stone hearth, the noise of the bustling cafe and its patrons, content with their surroundings, fades to a low murmur. As if Harvey (a friend you will come to know) himself snapped his fingers in front of my motionless face, I blink, and shake my head slightly to bring myself back to the present. I slowly gaze around the antique laden room from my vantage point sitting at a table in the back corner, like an outsider looking in. I imagine what it would be like to stop time for that moment and bring everyone, sharing this exact time and space, into a circle. Arm in arm, facing forward, with the windows of our souls wide-open, and standing equally in position; not one more prominent or important than the other. Wouldn't it be fascinating to find out who these people are, and most importantly, to share a glimpse of what they have endured in their lives? It might strike every one of us how we are all so similar and yet, our pasts are uniquely contrasting.

When we are mindlessly going through our day-to-day routines, numb to the world around us, and shut off from the feelings of others, do we truly live? Are we present in the moment, or are we mesmerized by an internal flame flickering and dying within us? Do we need a warm presence like Harvey within us all to snap fingers occasionally and bring us back to center? We robotically ask others how they are doing, and they do the same in return. The answer comes easy, "I am fine, thank you." But are we fine? I believe if you took the time to hear the truth behind the smiles and laughter, you would break down in sadness and weep for all humanity. You have no idea what others have endured, and you may never be privileged to know the whole story of their lives. Even if you yourself have been brutally broken, tread lightly and always be gentle.

Look around the next place you find yourself with a random gathering of people and ask yourself this: if we were all brought together in a circle, what could we learn from each other if the façade of, "I am fine, thank you." crumbled away? Contained within the following pages of this biography, Allen gives you a rare glimpse into his life with the windows to his soul wide-open. Standing arm in arm with you in the circle of life, he is sharing his most sacred secrets tucked behind his famous smile, songs, and laughter. Allen's heart is heavy, and his pain is real, so tread lightly and be gentle in your judgement, for he possesses something all humanity may be searching for. Now, after eighty-two years, this Country Gentleman is willing to share it all with you.

1

Light from Darkness

"You are not the darkness you endured. You are the light
that refused to surrender."
–Mark Green

Monday, June 10, 1940, at 4:56 a.m., just at the earliest stages of sunrise in Pottsville, Pennsylvania, the light separated from the darkness with the birth of a healthy baby boy. Cradled in the arms of the attending physician, Allen Karl Sterner spontaneously gasped his first breaths of life.[1] The first few breaths at birth are thought to be the most difficult ones your baby will take throughout its life. This certainly would not be the case for any child born from the womb of Katherine Mae "Kitty" Sterner.

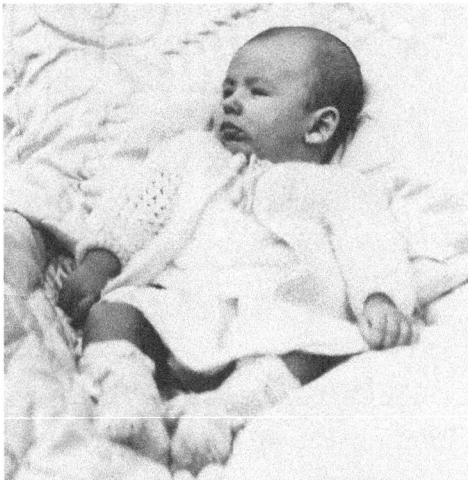

Allen Karl Sterner June, 1940

This cool summer day, wrought with wind and heavy rain, would be the day that she would never let her first-born son live down.[2] In the innocence of being born, he was now indebted for "ruining her life," and she would make her son pay in unimaginable ways. At the Lemos B. Warne Hospital, Allen's tiny footprints were inked and pressed for record on his Hollister Birth Certificate. His footprints, framed by his mother's right and left thumbprints, provided unchanging proof of identity throughout his life and forever linked Allen with his mother. These footprints would be the first of many that Allen would leave along his path to overcome, forgive, persevere, and become the light that separated from the darkness, illuminating the good in the world, and refusing to surrender.

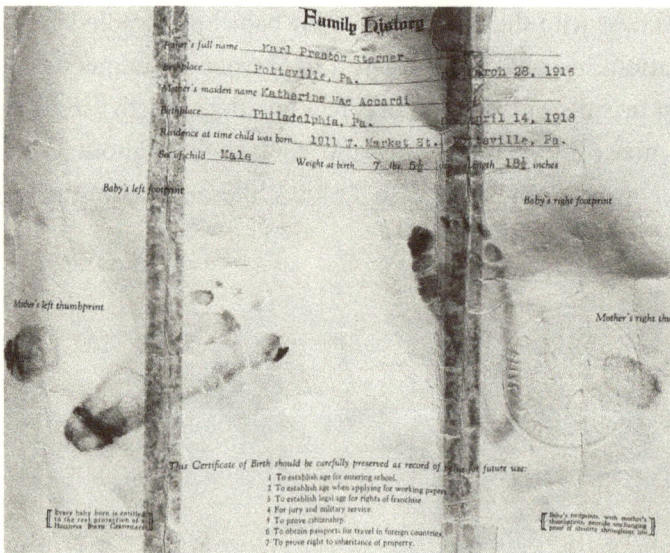

Backside of Allen's Birth Certificate

Babies born in the early morning hours grow up to be persistent by nature, contributing to their success.[3] They are intelligent and always prepared for any situation they might face, investing effort consistently until their dreams are achieved. Allen is a Gemini, the sign of the twins, characterized by curiosity, creativity, and confidence. His energy is a source of strength, support, and cooperative service. As a Gemini, Allen is among the most well-rounded, versatile, creative people on the planet. Feelings of genuine pleasure come from uplifting, teaching, and inspiring others. He does this by sharing his ideas in the most direct, positive, and honest manner possible. Caring words, expressed in song, build emotional bridges bringing constructive and emotional expression into the world. When stress, adversity, or trauma strikes, Allen can keep functioning physically and psychologically, despite experiencing deep anger, pain, and grief. He is resilient, and this attribute alone will prove to be the key to overcoming, forgiving, and forever breaking the cycle of abuse from which, he came.[4]

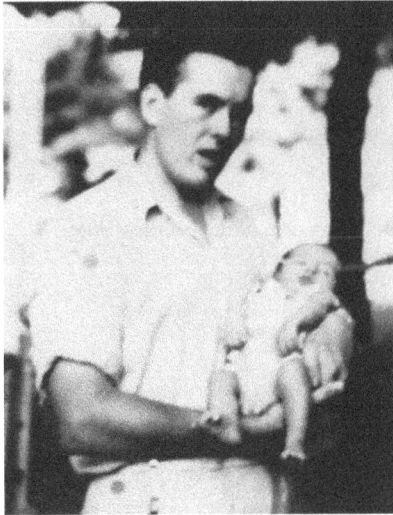

Karl holding Allen June 1940

Like all of us, Allen is ever changing and moving forward, but the experiences and people of his past forged him. The man he is today represents a culmination of past influences and decisions made along the way, both consciously and unconsciously. What is most important is not what happened to him, but what he purposely chose to take away from it all: not allowing his past to define his present or hold his future hostage.

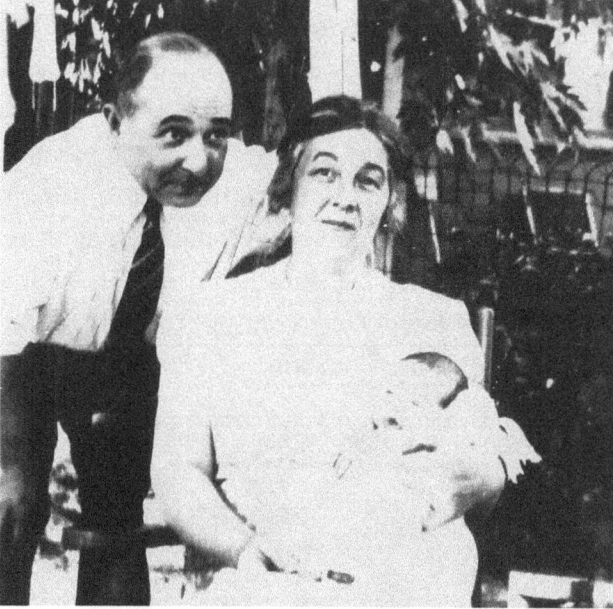

Pop and Nana holding Allen

2

Heritage

"As you walk down your path in life, you should endeavor to be an encouragement and inspiration to everyone you meet and leave them with the feeling that their lives are just a little better because you met. If you don't feel that you are doing that, then you must be on the wrong path."
–Francesco Accardi

Pop's immediate family in Sicily

In the early 1900s, the thriving economy of Pennsylvania drew a multitude of immigrants, especially from the poor and rural southern region of Italy. With little hope for progress and plagued by decades of internal conflict defined by violence, social chaos, and poverty, millions fled across the ocean in search of a better life.[5] The vast majority of these Italian immigrants were single young men like Allen's maternal grandfather, Francesco Accardi.

Seventeen-year-old Francesco "Frank" bravely set sail on the *Mendoza*, from the port of Palermo, on July 14, 1911. He left behind his parents and two sisters in Campobello di Mazara in Sicily, unaware he would never set foot back on his homeland again. With only a mandolin in hand and the word "hat" as his only spoken English word, Frank landed at Ellis Island. From there he made his way to Divernon, Illinois where extended family awaited to sponsor his stay. Determined to make something of himself, the young man began working in the Philadelphia area as a barber. Several years after settling in America, he heard the call of duty, and promptly joined the Army on April 15, 1918. Private Frank Accardi proudly served his new country during World War I in the Army's Medical Department located at Camp Lee in Virginia. Beating the odds of an estimated nine million killed in combat, Frank lived to return to his profession as a barber back home in Pennsylvania.[6]

His English steadily progressed as he urged people to correct him if he ever mispronounced or misused a word. Inspired by Dale Carnegie, an extremely successful man much like himself, he was unafraid of pursuing his dreams, rolling up his sleeves and working hard toward personal growth. As a result, Frank enrolled himself in the Dale Carnegie course titled, "How to Win Friends and Influence People," a move which would serve him well especially in business. Frank's favorite saying was, "It is far better to shoot high and knock the tail feathers off an eagle than it is to shoot low and kill a skunk."

Pvt. Francesco Accardi,
US Army WWI

As an outgoing and strapping, five feet, four inches tall, youthful man, he quickly caught the eye of the younger Pottsville native, Sarah May Haslam. Their attraction to one another resulted in a pregnancy, forever altering Frank's lifepath. In their day, news like this was scandalous, especially for a couple out of wedlock. Making things worse, Italians were exposed to widespread prejudice and racism. The term "WOP" was used frequently as a derogatory slang directed towards Italians standing for "Without Papers." Frank did not let this slur define or offend him. In every instance, where others called him a "WOP," his immediate response was, "I am sorry you feel that way because I would rather be friends."

Frank and Sarah weren't married until after the birth of their first daughter, Katherine Mae Accardi, in 1918. This fact would be a source of great embarrassment and a skeleton in the closet they wouldn't reveal even after their fiftieth wedding anniversary. Faced with a diagnosis of jaundice that forced a change in career, Frank secured a job with the Hoover Company where his sales skills and work ethic earned him the District Manager's position. With his quick thinking and charm, he oversaw product sales in five different states and could sell a vacuum to anyone. He once demonstrated the versatility of a

Hoover for a homemaker who didn't have a thread of carpeting in her home. When he showed her how the machine could vacuum the flies off the ceiling with one wave of the Hoover wand, she purchased the product on the spot.

Always wearing a nice suit and tie, Frank's impeccable style and wardrobe complimented his salesmanship. He obsessed over organization in every aspect of his life, spotlessly shining his shoes and separating them into perfect rows in an oversized armoire. He insisted on dry-cleaning his shirts with medium starch on hangers, and hung his socks, under shorts, and ties by color. When Frank strolled down the street, everyone who crossed his path knew his name and greeted him with the utmost respect. He earned a hefty salary of eighteen thousand dollars per year and in 1950, that kind of cash went a long way. This affluence afforded him the opportunity to provide for his family for years to come. In fact, Frank completely shouldered the responsibility of caring for his wife and three daughters, Katherine, Doris, and Jeanette, which is more than likely the reason he loved his Manhattan libations at the end of each day.

Sarah never aspired to be anything more than a homemaker and she fought ferociously with her husband, despising him for everything except his money. She never once drove a car, shopped for groceries, or paid bills, but she certainly adored spending Frank's money on the finer things. Generous to a fault, he doled out funds to his family for this or for that, even though he knew his wife had spending cash stashed away in her purse. It must be true that opposites attract because Sarah's disposition was nothing like the demeanor of her husband's. She was rude, foul mouthed, hateful, and mean spirited to her core. These were traits inevitably passed on to her daughter, Kitty. As dark as Sarah's disposition was, it paled in comparison to Kitty's profound immorality and wickedness that would make everyone's life she touched a living hell.

Allen's Mother, Grandmother and Great-Grandmother

3

Earliest Recollections

"I often go back to my earliest recollections and what I remember the most-my fourth birthday. My parents sang 'Happy Birthday' to me, but there was no cake, because my mother and father had a tough time surviving. My father was a carpenter, and my mother was a nervous wreck."
–Allen Karl Sterner

Pottsville, Pennsylvania is Allen's hometown. The discovery of a dense, high-energy coal in the late 1700s, and the establishment of an iron furnace along the banks of the Schuylkill River (Pronounced SKOO-Kil) prompted John Pott to found Pottsville, Pennsylvania in 1806. Formally laid out in 1816 and incorporated in 1828 with a strategic location on the river, it became the Schuylkill County seat in 1851.[7] Although the area is recognized primarily for its coal and textile industries, it is best known today for beer. Headquartered in the heart of Pottsville, Yuengling is the oldest brewery in the United States, established in 1829 by D.G. Yuengling & Son.[8]

Pottsville High School nicknamed "The Castle on the Hill," was where Allen's father, Karl Preston Sterner, fell in love with an undergraduate named Kitty. In her youth, Kitty was five feet, five inches tall, brown-haired, hazel-eyed, and petite beauty, appearing to be everything any young man could want. Karl was six feet one inches tall, and a stately looking man of German descent with dark-brown hair and deep brown, Omar Sharif-like, eyes.

Katherine "Kitty" Mae
Accardi Sterner Circa 1936

Karl Sterner Circa 1936

The couple seemed happy together in school, where times were more carefree. After graduating in 1935, Karl worked as a skilled carpenter, a trade his father LeRoy handed down to him. LeRoy Sterner was from Weissenberg, Germany. He was an exceedingly kind man who was enthusiastic about making homemade horseradish from a treasured family recipe. He married Karl's mother, Emma Louise, and together they raised their only son in a modest home at the corner of 1200 Howard Avenue in Pottsville. The narrow, three-story house was attached to a row of homes on one side and looked out across the street at a prominent town cemetery. In back there was a tapered, fenced in yard with a medium sized rabbit hutch at the far end. Guarding the confined area was a large, rust colored, sweet soul of a dog named Tango. Emma was a fantastic cook herself and made the world's best mashed potatoes.

At twenty-two years of age, Karl asked Kitty to be his wife and they were married by Reverend Weber on September 24, 1938. Apparently when filling out the application for a marriage license, Kitty should have replied, "YES" next to the question asking if she was of "unsound mind." The beginnings of a life of happily-ever-after with Karl fractured into unrecognizable pieces, undeserving of even being swept into the trash. Madness engulfed Kitty soon after the birth of their first son, and from that day forward, she referred to her baby boy as a "No-Good, German Bastard." Her explosive outbursts would convert any die-hard skeptic into a true believer in the possibilities of demonic possession.

Wedding Day September 24, 1938

I was always blamed for the fact that my mother was crazy now. She had a terrible time with my birth, and I was credited with everything wrong with her after that day. She let me know daily that if I hadn't been born, she would've been fine. I always felt bad about that, but no one asks to be born. So, here I was, and I was the problem. As a four-year-old, I certainly didn't know how to react to that, and I didn't know how to say, 'I am sorry for being born.' Obviously, I was sorry that I was ever born because it was an unbelievably dire situation for me.

Karl was the only parent who spent time with Allen and at the age of four, the boy recognized his father as the strength of the family and his mother as the weakness. She never provided a happy time because she was constantly upset, and it was nerve-racking.

Dad took me outside to our extended backyard to practice target shooting. At the age of four, I learned how to shoot a .22 rifle and pistol, and I fondly remember my dad being a very patient and loving man while teaching me.

Kitty with Allen Circa 1940

Winter fun with Dad

When Karl left the house for work each morning, it created an extremely uncomfortable situation because Allen found himself alone with a mother he didn't understand and didn't want to be with. She neglected to care for or even feed her son, leaving the four-year-old to fend for himself.

Most of the time I wasn't fed, but I knew putting pressure on my mom only made her scream louder at me. She didn't hit me back then, but she screamed at me, sending me running into my room to hide, because she was a raving maniac. Her carrying on was almost deafening. I didn't know what might happen next, so I tried to get away from it by hiding in a closet or under the bed. I'd say, 'Oh my God, Daddy! Please come home! Please Daddy, come home!' Unfortunately, my dad rarely got home in time to relieve the tension of the situation I found myself in.

Karl never had the luxury of turning down labor opportunities because his family struggled constantly with finances, only adding to the despair of the entire dysfunctional situation.

Mom never worked and Dad earned a meager wage, so we didn't have enough to eat. Dad fixed oatmeal for us, and I loved oatmeal, but not as often as we had to eat it. I was served oatmeal three times a day. I remember coming down the steps and looking through the railings to find oatmeal on the table, and I would just go back up to my room. Dad called out to me, 'Listen, you have to come down and eat. Come on down here!' Of course, when he ordered me down, I came to the table. I don't think my grandfather, whom I lovingly called "Pop-Pop," was aware that we had three servings of oatmeal every day. I never saw Pop give Mom money for groceries back then, but he did provide the roof over our heads, which she always expected.

Allen avoided his mother by offering to help his father with even the smallest of tasks.

Dad was a chain smoker and there was a cloud of smoke in the house because he never took it outside. I remember laying on the floor, stacking his little cigarettes as he made them. He put tobacco in this compact machine with paper and he rolled his own cigarettes, of course without filters. I stacked them as little logs and had a ton of fun doing that. At the same time, instead of smoking the cigarettes my dad just rolled, Mom tore each one apart to chew the tobacco inside. I remember them getting into arguments about that. 'Don't chew the tobacco, Kitty! You smoke it!' She was desperate for the instant flush of nicotine which chewing provided and couldn't resist tearing apart the cigarettes as quickly as I was stacking them up.

Allen's first sight of blood terrified him as he realized the mortality of the most important person in his life-his father. He was aware that he would be left alone with his mother if anything ever happened to him, and she was the one person he wanted to stay away from. To Allen, his mother became a very scary person.

Dad had a bandsaw in the basement where he crafted different things for me. One time, he was making a wooden toy gun and cut himself very badly on that saw. He jumped back and I intuitively knew he was hurt, although he never communicated this to me. He grabbed his hand and ran upstairs leaving behind a trail of bright red blood. I ran right after him and felt so badly that he was hurt, especially while making something for me. There was no money for a doctor's care, so he held his bloodied hand under the faucet in the kitchen sink, wrapped it, and took care of the wound himself.

Allen remembers the kindness of his paternal grandparents, LeRoy and Emma Sterner, and reminiscing on his rare visits with them brings a smile to his face. These special times as a young boy made an impression and offered a welcomed reprieve from the unsettling times at home. It was also his first encounter with animals as pets and the unconditional love they express that sparked a life-long appreciation for all living things.

I visited my dad's parents before the age of four, and the thing I remembered most was grandma's mashed potatoes. Despite my best efforts, I've never been able to make mashed potatoes the way Emma Sterner could. She was this little, gray-haired, lady with a neat bun on the back of her head. She always held me on her lap and sang German songs to me. My grandfather LeRoy used to take me by the hand and lead me down to the end of the yard where he kept pet rabbits in a hutch. They also owned a dog that I loved, and this dog loved me. We sat next to each other, and I'd pet him. We wrestled and played on the carpet, and eventually fell asleep together. His name was Tango and I wish I knew whatever happened to him. Those were such special times, even though the only time I ever got to visit them was when my dad would take me there.

Emma and brother Barney
with Allen and dog, Tango

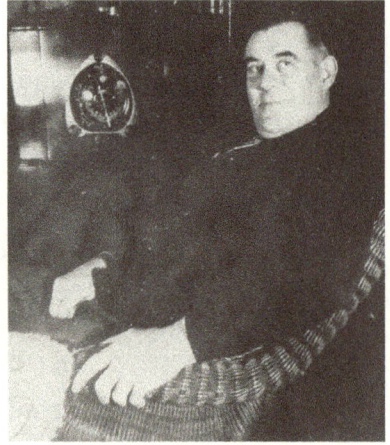

Paternal grandfather LeRoy Sterner

With less than fifteen hundred days on earth, little Allen's life was severely lacking the safety, stability, and nurturing that every child requires for healthy development. The physical neglect and emotional abuse were just the beginning of the adverse childhood experiences Allen would face.

4

Walking Away

*"Leaving without explanation constitutes the most wounding
of goodbyes, which no child ever forgets."*
–Julie Richardson

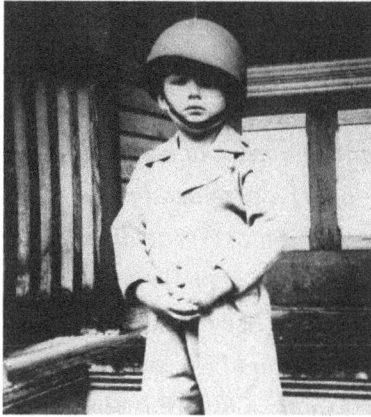

Battleworthy
Wearing Johnny Garrigan's helmet

Allen's mother was constantly distressed, and the verbal abuse
was chipping away at whatever bond of love she once shared
with her husband. When Karl wasn't working to support his family,
he was home dealing with an unloving wife who failed at being a
good mother to their son. Kitty's tirades and emotional and physical
outbursts became increasingly difficult to deal with, leaving Karl
desperate for help.

> *Dad took Mom to see the doctor, because she was a raving
> maniac and he needed help with her. She wouldn't consent to
> it, but she obviously needed treatment. While driving, Dad held*

her down on the floorboard between the dash and the front seat, preventing her from jumping out of our moving car. I sat in the back seat of this 1940s car while all the commotion was happening, and it was a very traumatic situation. I always knew he was in complete control, but it was all certainly beyond me as a child.

Kitty constantly found fault with Karl because he couldn't do the things she wanted. He truly gave it his best effort, but nonetheless, her frustrations escalated her verbal abuse into physical violence.

I remember the terrible arguments between my parents, and I would retreat into a corner and cover my ears because their voices were so loud. She yelled at him, but I don't ever remember my dad hitting her. I do remember how, oh my gosh, that woman slapped and hit him repeatedly in the face. In return he simply grabbed her by the upper arms and pressed them firmly against her body telling her repeatedly, 'That's enough! That's enough!' It was terrible and I felt so badly for him. I wanted him to hit her back, but he never did. He never did! He simply walked away from her and all the while she would be hitting him on the back. I wish he would have hit her because she was mistreating the one person, I felt closest to. My dad was the one person in my life that seemed like he cared for me. I thought that was special and I felt close to him, because at the time, I didn't feel like I had anyone else in the world who cared about me.

Karl was a gifted carpenter, and a talented trumpet player. He won local contests playing the song, 'Flight of the Bumblebee,' which any trumpet player can tell you is no walk in the park to play. Karl was a member of the non-profit, 3rd Brigade Band. With its origins in the Civil War, this band traditionally played for every special event in town.[9] On the side, Karl put together a four-piece band with his best friend and trombone player, Johnny. Allen fondly remembers the times he spent with this jovial man whenever he visited.

Karl Sterner in his Pottsville
High School Band Uniform

Johnny Garrigan
and Raggs Circa 1944

Dad's band practiced at our house, and I enjoyed listening because the music was fantastic. Johnny was one of his absolute best friends and he was the sort of guy that if you met him, you loved him. He had an outgoing personality, and I cherished the fact that he played with me, and we had so much fun together. He came to our house quite often and spent most of his time with me. He even tried to teach me how to play his trombone. We played Hide-and-Seek and other fun games. I thought it was so great when he let me wear his WWII Army helmet and took my picture out in front of our house. He made me laugh and I was so happy because he shielded me from my mom while he was there. Johnny kept me from having to cower in my closet or under my bed and made every ounce of unhappiness provoked with her ranting and raving disappear. He was my guardian and I looked up to him like I looked up to my dad. When we weren't playing, it seemed like he was always going upstairs to my mom's bedroom to calm her down from being this rage of a person.

Kitty was terribly unhappy with Karl's lack of ability to provide for her and his absence from the house grew longer and more frequent as he stressed over making ends meet. Kitty's revelation of a second pregnancy intensified the fighting between them which now centered around the suspicion of infidelity.

Mom gave birth to another baby boy when I was four and a half years old and the terrible arguments that happened between my parents worsened. I didn't know what to do, so I just held tightly to my dad's leg while they were hollering at one another. I was terrified because I didn't know if somebody was going to get hurt and it was just a terrible time for a child my age to live through. I remember being so scared that I wanted to stick by my dad, because he was the one person who could protect me. The screaming was ear splitting between them one morning. Mom stood at the top of the stairs, and we were standing at the bottom. Mom was carrying on and had the baby carriage upstairs with my little brother, Jerry Lynn Sterner laying in it. She continued yelling down to him about the baby, and he was hollering back at her when suddenly, she shoved the baby carriage down the steps towards us.

The carriage tumbled downward, and I can still see that tiny newborn baby leaving the carriage as it smashed against the wall behind us. Dad moved me out of harm's way and snatched the baby out of midair! It was like the greatest football reception in history. He righted the carriage and carefully placed the baby back in it. Without another word, he picked me up, hugged me, and walked out the front door.

Stairwell Scene – Sketch by Geoffrey Beadle

Still traumatized from the morning's events, Allen was sleepless and yearning for his father's return. Karl did return to the house that night, but he didn't come back for Allen or Jerry.

I was lying awake when my dad came home in the middle of the night. Mom was sleeping and didn't know a thing about it. He crept into my bedroom, gathered me up in his arms, and carried me downstairs. We sat together while he packed his carpentry tools into his handmade, wooden toolbox. When he finished, he hugged and kissed me as he carefully placed me back in my bed. He whispered, 'Go to sleep now.' He didn't know it, but I climbed out of bed and looked down through the stair railing at him. I watched as he put his toolbox over his shoulder and walked out the front door and out of my life. Over the years, he never tried to get back in touch with me and that hurt me deeply. At the time he walked away, he drove this 1940s Chevy Coupe, and on the back of his car trunk was a red piece of rubber sticking out. He had the rubber there to keep the moisture from leaking into his trunk. I identified his car by that piece of rubber and for weeks after he left, I searched for his car. I climbed onto our sofa, leaned over, and peered out the window studying the trunk of every car that drove by. At times, I was desperate to spot that red rubber piece, but I never saw his car again. Although as a child I was certain he'd come back for me one day, he never did. I've always wondered what my life would be like if he had come back that night for me and Jerry and not just to retrieve his beloved carpentry tools.

On Dad's Lap Circa 1944

Shortly after Karl took off, a letter surfaced in the family that was presented as being written and sent by him. The hand-written letter was addressed to Pop and implied that Karl was headed elsewhere to look for work so he could send money back to his family. In this letter he asked Pop to take care of his babies in his absence. Allen never believed his father penned such a letter. Instead, he highly suspected that his mother wrote it to hide the truth. Whoever it was, they weren't very well educated because it was full of grammatical mistakes and words that were scratched out in various places. The letter read as follows:

Dear Pop,

I am taking your suggestion of June, when you remember you told me to go away and get work and you would promise to take good care of Kitty and the babies. Well Pop as you know things can't go on this way for ever and you are running in debt with the house and all. This way I can send money home for Kitty and the kids and pay their way that way.

Pop you gave me your word you would take care of them for God's sake do that and I'll take care for my end This is damn site harder to do than you think especially around the holidays I hope you understand this problem and bear with me.

If necessary, close the house and take them home as you said you would and rent the house. In that way we can still make a go of it later.

Go to Rev. Weber if you need help with Kitty and babies, he will help no end.

Give my love to my wife and little babies try to make them understand it's for the best and I'll send money as soon as I get a pay. That won't be long about a week or so. God bless you and mom and everyone I'll miss you all.

Yours with the utmost respect

Karl

The letter was analyzed in 2021 by two different handwriting experts. Both professionals concluded that Karl didn't write the letter but nor did Kitty. After seventy-six years, it was determined that the handwriting sample matched that of Sarah. More than likely, Allen's maternal grandmother created the letter to cover up Kitty's infidelities and even the state of her daughter's mental instability. Pop held company with city officials and judges and could sway legal matters whenever necessary. So, in the Court of Common Pleas in Schuylkill County there was a legal notice posted in 1946. The notice intended to notify Karl that his wife was "praying a divorce" from him and called on him to appear in court. The default of such an appearance would render him liable to have the divorce granted in his absence. It is unknown if Karl showed in court that day as requested, but regardless, Allen's parents were now officially divorced, and Kitty didn't waste any time setting her sights on someone new.

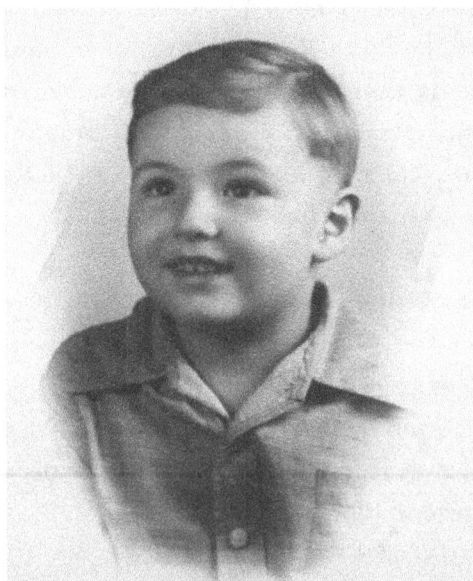

Allen 1944

5

Cruel and Unusual Punishment

"How do you forgive the people who were supposed to protect you?"
–Courtney Summers

After Karl walked out, the now three-hundred-and-fifty-pound Kitty was a total physical and mental wreck. Frank and Sarah explored treatment options for their daughter, and a close friend recommended a man named George Jones. George was a self-proclaimed naturalist living in the nearby town of Schuylkill Haven. He was certain that he could help Kitty with her mental condition and so she moved in with George and left her two boys behind in Pottsville. For the next two years, Allen and Jerry went without a single phone call or personal visitation with their mother, leaving them to wonder if she was still living. After the divorce, LeRoy and Emma were forbidden to see their grandsons and now the care of these two young boys was left solely up to Kitty's parents. After raising three children of her own, Sarah didn't want the responsibility of caring for Allen or Jerry and was outwardly upset with the inconvenience of it all. Allen called his grandmother "Nana," but there was nothing grandmotherly about her. Life under her watch was regimented and never once did she hold the boys on her lap, read to or play games with them.

Living with my grandparents for two years was a very trying time because Nana didn't want us there and never showed us loving kindness. I never felt welcomed or that she was ever glad we were there. I often heard my brother crying in his crib and when I mentioned it to Nana, she ignored me and just let him cry. Being a kid myself, I didn't know what to do and this always bothered me because she wasn't paying any attention to my baby brother's needs.

Before moving in with Pop and Nana Circa 1945

As soon as Pop left for work in the morning, Sarah tied Allen underneath the kitchen table for the greater part of the day. His small ankle was tied with a twisted piece of bed sheet to the leg of a gray and white, 1940s era table. She expected the child to entertain himself with the few toys she threw under there to play with. One of the toys Allen interacted with the most was a large, stuffed teddy bear which he repeatedly punched. Working out his frustrations, he stood the bear up against the table leg and punched it repeatedly, then pushed the bear to the floor and did it again. Being tied under a table for that length of time also gave him the chance to memorize every detail. It was a porcelain topped, metal, gray and white table with two side leaves pressed down and stored directly beneath the top. These leaves measured approximately fifteen inches wide and were spring-loaded which allowed them to be pulled out and popped up automatically into place.

My grandparents never ate at this table. It was just a worktable for my grandmother while she puttered in her kitchen. She only ever pulled up the one leaf closest to the kitchen sink leaving the other side flush against the wall. When I napped under there, I would lie on my back and look up at the underside of the table. I studied every feature, and it was startling to me to watch the leaf mechanism work the way they did. I was tied in place for the entire day unless I had to get up to use the restroom. As soon as I finished, Nana immediately tied me back under there. Although Nana spent most of her day standing near me, she didn't bother to interact with me in any way.

Pop and Nana's house was kept like a museum and Nana was very fussy and possessive of all her knick knacks. Anything moved, even the slightest bit, she would obsessively reposition it and insist on being the last one to touch it. The living room was roped off and although you could peek into the room, no one was allowed to enter except one time a year-on Christmas Day. Pop hired a regular house cleaner named Sadie who talked to Allen while he was sitting under the table, but she never once thought to untie him or report this unthinkable treatment to the authorities.

I don't think Pop was ever made aware of Nana's cruelty towards us. When he came home from work to have lunch, Nana would move us into the basement and hold us silently under the stairs. I could hear Pop's shoes walking across the floor above us, but we weren't allowed to make even the slightest sound. Oh, how I wanted to be with my grandfather. Pop came home every day at the same time for lunch and like clockwork we were rushed to the basement. Nana held her hand tightly over Jerry's mouth so he wouldn't cry out, and his eyes went wide, and face turned blue. She simply wanted her husband to come and go from the house as quickly as possible and if he knew we were there, he would linger to spend time with us. He could never have imagined we were there under the basement stairs all along. He would have been irate about that. Nana never hit me or cussed at me, but she yanked me around by my arm and made the ugliest face, scaring the heck out of me. I never did anything to provoke her because I was trained to be fearful and keep my mouth shut. Knowing I was going to be with her for God knows how long, I learned to be quiet and cooperative. Fear kept me this way and I thought, 'Tomorrow is another day and I want to live to see it.'

The day that Allen most wanted to live to see each week was Sunday. Nana wouldn't drive a car herself, but on the weekends, she demanded her husband take everyone in his large Hudson to visit family and friends. Fred and Laura Williams, along with their daughter Darlene, were visited the most because Laura and Sarah were related as part of the extensive Haslam family. This made young Darlene and Allen distant fourth cousins. Although Darlene was three years younger than Allen, they got along very well and the two became inseparable; playing games and coloring together.

Darlene would take her crayons away from me because I was mashing down the point. She had a nice light way of coloring that saved the point of the crayon, and I pressed down on them too hard because I wanted my coloring to look deeper and brighter. She pulled the crayons away from me and her mother Laura said, 'Darlene, you can't do that.' Darlene would exclaim, 'Well, look what he did to my crayons!' Darlene taught me how to color and save the points by slightly rolling each crayon to the side as I stroked.

Coloring in a way that preserves the point of the crayon isn't the only important thing Darlene would teach Allen during his visits. There were many positive outcomes from interacting with one another, but the farthest-reaching lesson came from a photo of a man Darlene's family had proudly hanging on the wall.

I noticed a picture hanging on Darlene's wall of a man with a beard and long hair. I didn't recognize this person, so I asked Darlene about it. 'I've never seen this man before, is he a relative of yours?' Surprised, Darlene said, 'Oh my gosh, no! That's Jesus! You don't know Jesus?' I had never been to church, and I didn't even know how to pray, so I had no idea who Jesus was. Darlene's mother heard this and asked Pop if it would be all right to take me with them to the Seventh Day Adventist camp meetings where I could learn more about this man called Jesus. If I was with Darlene, it was a fun time, so I looked forward to joining them.

These meetings were world-wide Crusades for Christ and a special time, because I met a lot of different people, and they were so kind to me. Everyone smiled and cared about each other, which was certainly something I wasn't used to. Participants brought a dish to share and there were other activities such as church picnics and softball games. I was starting to have fun for the first time in my life. These Crusades were wonderful with animated ministers who didn't just stand behind the pulpit and preach. They moved around the stage and delivered the message of God in compelling ways, encouraging their parishioners to call on God directly should they ever need His help. My most enduring memory of these camp meetings was listening to evangelists, Ray Turner and Dick Barron sing the hymn, 'Mansion Over the Hilltop.' With their beautiful baritone and tenor voices in perfect harmony, at just six years old, I was mesmerized and wished that their song, and that day would never end.

At that time, there was no kindergarten level of school so six-year-old Allen attended first grade at Yorkville Elementary. His favorite teacher of all time was Ms. Gray because she was an excellent teacher who treated Allen, and every other student, as if they were her very own children. At the end of the first-grade year, Ms. Gray brought the entire class up to the second-grade classroom where she pointed out the ABCs on the wall. They too would learn their ABC's during the following school year, but unfortunately, Allen would never attend the second grade there. By this time, Nana was sick and tired of caring for the boys and decided it was time to ship them back to their mother. Allen had just turned seven and Jerry was a toddler when they reunited with Kitty, and by this time, she was married to George Jones. The couple lived together with his father Clayton Henry Jones "Pop Jones" on a farm in the country. A sprawling four-hundred-thirty-acres located in rural Schuylkill County, Pennsylvania. It consisted of dense woods, lush pastures, a pond and stream, farmhouse, two barns, a pig stable, and a two-car detached garage. Eventually they added an old work horse and two thousand free-roaming chickens.

We moved into this large haunted looking, old farmhouse where the entire backside was caved in with dirt. The heavy rains caused a mudslide which knocked everything in leaving it wide open to the elements. Racoons, possums, poisonous snakes, mice, flies, and dozens of cats and dogs could find their way in at night and wander around freely. There was no heat, electricity, inside toilet, or running water. Even worse, my mom was no better off mentally for having been treated at the farm for those two years.

After his wife, Annie Fehr Jones, passed away in 1942 at the age of fifty-nine, Pop Jones resided in the farmhouse attic above their son George, his new wife Kitty, and now her two young boys. The attic was bare and rudimentary without insulation, drywall, or climate control. The summers were boiling hot, raising the temperature to over one hundred degrees in the poorly ventilated space, where the war on wasps raged daily. Wasps managed to enter through one of the many cracks in the walls and made their way to the light of the window where they met a cruel fate. Pop Jones was an iron horse with hands tough as nails. Built up with callouses upon calluses, his scarred hands bore evidence of sixty plus years of arduous work. Despite ineffective efforts to sting, wasps were squashed between his thumb and index finger and their lifeless bodies tossed to the floor. Poisonous copperhead snakes were no match for this country barbarian either, as he was quick to catch them behind their head and twist it around until it finally pulled right off.

Step-father George Jones with Allen
and Jerry on the PA farm

Pop Jones was a lanky, tall, ragged, and gaunt looking man in his late sixties. His clothing over his long underwear was dated and filthy.

Suspenders held up his baggy, wrinkled, and soiled wool pants, with their top button missing. His leather boots were scuffed and thin of sole, and his cotton shirt was buttoned to the very top of his neck, with the sleeves rolled high for work. His vintage railroad hat was always on his silver-haired head, as if paying sad homage to days gone by. It was rankly evident that he rarely bathed or washed his clothes. His face was never clean shaven, but scruffy, with a stubble of a white beard. On the side of his head grew a substantial cancerous tumor that bled and festered continuously. Without indoor plumbing, Pop Jones would make his way to the creek five times a day, lay on his side, and splash water up on the tumor to clean it. He was rough on the outside, but kind on the inside, and he took a liking to Allen who was always impressed with the things that this man could do.

Pop Jones with Allen and Jerry on the PA farm Circa 1947

For hours each day, Pop Jones would take off walking in the woods and oh, how Allen wished he could go exploring with him. Sadly, he couldn't just take off for the day because his farm chores were plentiful, and his mother was meaner now than ever. She never wanted her boys back and her frustration played out in unimaginable ways. The blatant neglect of Allen and Jerry would leave invisible scars far worse than any outward lashing she could ever deliver.

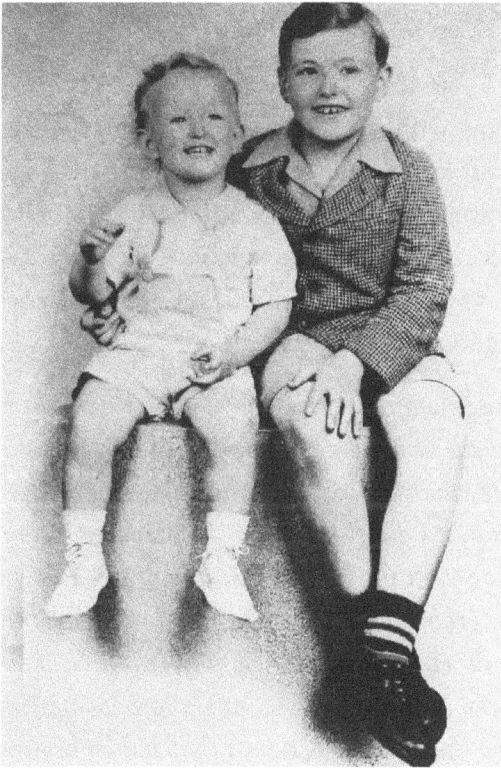

Allen and Jerry Circa 1947

6

Mommy's Just Nervous

*"Life is not about how hard of a hit you can give, it's about
how many you can take and still keep moving forward."*
–Sylvester Stallone (Rocky)

After staying with their grandparents for two years, Allen and
Jerry didn't know their mother any more than she knew them.
Kitty was as upset to receive her children back as their grandmother
was glad to get rid of them. The welcome back began with a vicious
beating unleashed on Allen, the first of many he would have to
endure throughout his boyhood.

*She made something to eat, and I didn't care for the way it
looked, but she ordered me to eat it anyway. I tentatively tasted
a small bite while she glared at me, and apparently, I gave the
impression that I didn't like what she prepared. Mom slammed
her fists down on the table and came around to where I was
sitting. She grabbed me by my hair and pulled me right off the
kitchen chair. Her physical attacks are hard to explain. I mean,
it was thirty to forty-five seconds of a beating you couldn't
believe; like the mauling of a bear that suddenly grabs you and
bam, bam, bam, bam! So fast and brutal as if I were struck by
lightning. I thought, 'What the heck just happened? What is the
crime in not liking what she fixed?' She kept hitting me and all
heaven and hell came together because I never expected it. I knew
from that point on, she had a hair-trigger temper, and the slightest
little thing could set her off and you better watch out.*

She wouldn't stop hitting me until she hurt her hand, and every time she hit my skull, I knew it hurt her. She would give a couple of last punches and when she let go, I dropped limp to the floor. She would only strike with her fists or hands and never used a paddle, switch, or other object to hit me. As an adult, I rationalized that she wanted to feel her fist and hand on me. I think when a person does that, they are letting you know you are worthless and absolutely mean nothing to them. A paddle or switch is what you remember hurting you and not the person. The fist is up close and personal. Mom wanted to personally deliver the pain to me.

The attacks on Allen would not only inflict physical and mental pain, but leave behind awful bleeding from his nose, ears, and mouth. The bruising was severe enough to swell his eyes completely shut, so to see where he was walking, Allen used his small fingers to pry open his eyelids. Not having sight after the beatings brought a dreadful feeling of vulnerability over him, because he couldn't observe and correct any issues which might trigger another fit of rage.

On the farm, I learned to watch Mom's facial expressions as she scanned the room, and I anticipated anything that might upset her to the point of losing control. I had to always predict her responses to everything. Being this observant and initiative-taking was way beyond what a seven-year-old child should have to think about. I wanted to survive and so I learned, and it trained me to take care of things immediately. There are people in the military that aren't even this well trained. 'I got it Mom. Yes, I see it. I got it!' I did that every single day. I knew if she was unhappy, then we would pay for it.

You don't know how many times I wished I were that little boy tied up underneath Nana's kitchen table again because at least I was fed and never hit to the point where I wondered if I was going to wake up the next day. I had a strict existence there, but I didn't live in terror. It was predictable which was easier than the uncertainty I faced each day at the hands of my mom. She was only loving to me after she beat the heck out of me. After a few hours or days, she called me to her and said, 'You know Mommy wouldn't have done this if she wasn't nervous. You understand, 'Mommy's just nervous?' What was I going to say to her? 'That's a lie!' The last thing I was going to do was disagree with her so without expression, and in a monotone voice, I repeated, 'I understand Mom. Yes, I understand.'

Nana Accardi with Allen and Jerry
at the PA farm

Unfortunately, Allen's grandparents threw him back into the lion's den and there was no one in the world he could turn to for preservation. His grandparents, aunts and uncles all lived within an hour drive from the farmhouse, but they may as well have lived on another continent as visits were rare. Even the adults occupying the same house, ignored the abuse that Kitty unleashed. Pop Jones went out of his way to keep to himself in the attic or stay out in the woods to avoid the craziness.

George Jones was born in September of 1906. He was a five feet nine inches tall, one hundred-and-twenty-two -pound, meek man born without a mean bone in his body. George had blue eyes which accented his pale complexion and light-brown hair. He was soft spoken, peaceful, God loving, and the most angel like man you could ever imagine. A self-proclaimed naturalist, without any credentials whatsoever, he tried to sell natural remedies out of a storeroom, but the house was so far removed from town that very few customers patronized the place.

He was there with Allen and Jerry, but he was unable to do anything about anything. He couldn't stand up to Kitty on even the smallest of issues and ended up as just another one of the poor souls victimized in her whirlpool of madness.

George helped me to walk around after the beatings when I couldn't see, and sometimes even brought me a wet washcloth for my face. Sadly, he never spoke out against it because my mom attacked him too. She hit and punched him in the face until he bled and all he said was, 'Oh hon, oh hon, oh stop!' I strongly wished he could have knocked her out or knock her to the floor and beat the heck out of her, but he never did. She was a deranged maniac who never got better, and I watched all of this unfold and thought, 'Here we go again. I am back in the woods and there's no escape.' She never stopped calling me a "No-Good German Bastard." Dad left her, and I was the product of that, so apparently in her twisted mind, I had to pay with my life.

Although George was submissive to Kitty's attacks, with each beating she unleashed on the family, he devised eyebrow raising treatments to heal her.

Mom wasn't calmer for having stayed with George and enduring his therapeutic treatments which he took very seriously. His marriage to my mom was his only one in his lifetime and I felt like he genuinely loved her and wanted her to get better. Poor George always tried to get her under control, and there is no doubt that she was the biggest challenge of his career. He conducted various therapy sessions to heal her nervous condition, especially after she lost control and punched me. He tried such things as making her sit naked in a farm animal water trough filled with cold water or in an enormous hand-dug hole behind our detached garage.

Therapy – Sketch by Geoffrey Beadle

Precise dimensions were important to George, so the hole had to be twelve feet deep and six by six feet, squared. For several straight weeks, he pulled out bucket after bucket of dirt and piled it high on the sides. At each corner he deliberately placed sixteen-foot, solid copper rods down in the hole. Each rod was a half inch in diameter with a large brass knob on the end and it looked like a Star Wars kind of thing. He believed in the grounding properties of the earth and its therapeutic properties with its own energy field. This strong magnetic field was supposed to calm her down and offer her some relief from her episodes. George then placed a wooden ladder into the hole, let Mom descend into it, then immediately removed the ladder leaving her sitting there for several hours at a time.

Carefully approaching the hole, I looked down through my pried open and swollen eyes, to see my morbidly obese mother sitting there in the middle of the hole, right on the dirt, stark naked. I must admit that at times, I thought about pushing the dirt on top of her because I just knew that if I trapped her down there, I would never receive another beating. There were times I thought of her as the enemy and self-preservation took over and I just wanted to survive. I never thought of killing my mom because honestly, a kid doesn't think about that. You're simply trying to protect yourself and stop the next attack. I truthfully thought, 'If she could go to the hospital, it would be a relief and the much-needed time out from her viciousness to heal.' Whatever it took, but I sure needed the beatings to stop. When allowed to resurface, Mom was no better off. She was still a raving maniac, and it was left up to me to play psychiatrist to this sick woman.

As the weekly beatings increased in intensity, Allen's closest ally, Darlene, began taking notice.

Going back and living with my mom was an unwise decision, but it wasn't up to me. She punished me very badly and I displayed extensive swelling on my face and most of my body was black and blue. When Pop picked me up at the farm to visit the Haslam family, Darlene immediately noticed the swelling and bruising, but I always made excuses like I had fallen out of a tree, or I fell off my bike. Maybe tripped and fell while running, but after a while, Darlene thought something wasn't right that I kept falling and tripping. To keep myself from looking like a clumsy idiot, I finally confided in Darlene and told her the truth about how my mom abused me. Darlene was a feisty little thing and she said, 'Well, I'm going to tell my mother and she's going to talk to your mother, and this will stop!' I panicked! 'No, no, no, you can't do that! Do you wanna get me killed? She'll kill me, Darlene! Please don't tell!' Luckily, I convinced her that she needed to keep my secret, and she did. She kept my secret for years and I trusted and respected her for doing so. Not once did I think that she and I would be married someday and spend fifty-one years connected to one another. I honestly never gave that a thought.

If a child could notice the marks of abuse and question it, why didn't the adults in contact with Allen question the same thing? Out of all the adults who interacted with him, it was only his Pop who asked if his mother was hurting him.

Pop came to the farm more frequently than any of my other family members. Although Mom was his flesh and blood, he began to realize after months of seeing me bruised, bloodied, and swollen, that there was something happening. He drove out to the farm to give me and Jerry our haircuts and upon seeing undeniable excessive swelling and bruising on my face and body, he finally asked, 'What happened? What's going on here?' Without skipping a beat, I lied telling him how I fell out of a tree, encountered poison sumac – any excuse I could think of to defuse the situation. What was I supposed to do, testify against his own flesh and blood? He finally asked me directly while driving me home one day, 'Is your mother mistreating you?' 'No, Pop! No, heck no! She's not hurting me!' What I so desperately wanted to

say was, 'I am going to tell you the truth, Pop, but you must
promise me that you will keep driving, turn the corner, and get
me out of here. If you're not going to do that then, 'No, Pop!
Mom's not hurting me.'

The attitude towards children in the 1940s and 1950s was one of
children should be seen and not heard. If a child was struck by their
parent, it was because they deserved it and the blame was placed
directly on the child for misbehaving. There weren't school counselors
or child protective services, and families didn't meddle in each other's
affairs when it came to managing their own.[10] Also, no one expected
this woman to be an abuser. Kitty was the life of the party and her act
of being a loving mother when others were around was Oscar worthy
to say the least. Smiling, dancing, laughing and full of life, everyone
believed that Allen was the luckiest kid on earth to have such a good
mother to raise him.

Mom was a socialite, and if anyone came by the house to visit,
she turned into a person I didn't recognize. She was a smiling,
jovial, and welcoming saint. Yet, as soon as that front door shut,
a cloud came over her and she was instantly back to her hideous
ways. With visitors, I had to be careful of what was said, and if
I had bruises, then I had to make excuses. She'd glance at me
like don't you even say a word and I knew if I did say something,
when everyone left, I was in for it. I played the role perfectly,
telling them how much I loved my mom, which she desperately
needed people to hear. They commented on how good looking I
was and how I will have girls after me one day. I was forced to
respond, 'No, my mother is the only one I want to be with. I'm
never gonna get married, I'm never gonna have a girlfriend.'
People didn't want to accept that, and they argued. I wanted to
kick them in the shin and say, 'Stop saying I am lucky to have
such a wonderful mother!'

It wasn't until Allen was grown that he realized Pop, nor any other adult in his life, never really wanted to remove him and Jerry from their neglectful situation. They didn't want to take on the responsibility of raising two young boys themselves and Nana already made it clear that she no longer wanted to look after the boys.

Pop loved me, but I knew he would always be biased because my mom was his daughter and he loved her very much and would do anything for her. I didn't think that he would completely believe that I was being beaten like that. I knew that I couldn't count on him, and he was the one person that fed me, gave me love, taught me everything he knew, and at the same time, he was still my mom's father.

By superficially caring, asking about, and Allen openly denying the obvious, Pop was now off the hook. If he didn't testify against his mother, then the abuse must not be happening. Pop was no longer responsible for correcting his daughter's evil acts and he could continue to focus on his success and image as the great American dreamer. Although Pop tried to have influence in the quality of life for his grandsons with monetary gifts, groceries, and farm help, it was all only a shear and makeshift band aid over a heinous injustice happening right under his nose.

Allen's family and friends ignoring the obvious signs of physical abuse, excused by Kitty's nervous condition, only fanned the flames, and flung the door wide open for the unspeakable that was forthcoming.

7

Harvey, Are You Okay?

"From dark clouds we get precious water. From dark mines
we get valuable jewels. And from our darkest trials
come our best blessings from God."
–Unknown

A llen accepted and adapted to the deplorable conditions he lived
in on the farm because he came from being tied underneath a
kitchen table and had no preconceived notion of what life should be
like for a child. Children can't miss something they never had in
the first place. It wasn't the neglectful living conditions that made
life difficult for Allen as much as it was the avoidance of his mother's
fury and the anticipation of her every need. Kitty was helpless and
demanding regarding every household task, especially baking or
cooking. Obese and lazy, she sat at the kitchen table barking out the
ingredients and culinary tools she needed to suddenly appear before
her. Nervously, Allen scurried to meet his mother's every demand
and when finished, every bit of the kitchen clean up fell upon his
shoulders.

Utterly overwhelmed with pleasing his mother and helping
with chores on the farm, at seven years old, Allen was also the sole
caregiver to his two-and-a-half-year-old brother. Every single day,
Allen saw to it that Jerry was bathed, dressed, fed, and looked after
because Kitty couldn't be bothered to do it. Experiencing first-hand
the severity of his mother's beatings, Allen did everything in his
power to keep his little brother safe from her. Jerry was small with a

frail body and Allen worried that his mother would kill him with her maliciousness. Observing her every expression, Allen immediately sensed when she was about to lose control and take her frustrations out on Jerry. Instinctively, big brother moved in to protect him by taking the extra blows himself.

She didn't hurt my brother very often because I protected him. He was really my child to raise, and he was so frail. I was the husky one and I was built big, and he was this weakened little boy. If she thought he did something wrong, I'd say, 'No, Mom! No, it was me, not Jerry!' I knew that there was no way he could have taken her hits like I could. I think she would have hurt him and may have even killed him because she didn't realize how hard she was hitting. Or she did, but she couldn't stop once she got started. Jerry feared her. Sometimes he would do the simplest of things like leaving his toys out on the floor and she lost control screaming, 'Who did this?' Jerry fled to the corner and just folded, and I took the hit. We both knew it was his fault, but I had to protect him. One time, she grabbed him by his thin arms and thumped him in the middle of the back. It sounded like a hollow drum and Jerry went flying across the room. I don't know how she didn't break his little frame of a body that day.

Allen was now enduring up to three beatings per week and wondering what it would feel like to die. In his heart, he knew he couldn't survive another violent attack and deeply craved the same love, care, and protection he provided for his baby brother. Allen recalled the sermons from the camp meetings he attended with Darlene and her family, and it gave him strength.

Mom always cursed me saying, 'God damn you! God damn you!' During the camp meetings, there was nothing they said that made me believe God would damn me, so it no longer had any meaning for me. Her words lost power in my mind. I was told repeatedly at the camps that if I ever needed help, I should ask God directly. I believed with all my heart God would help me if I needed him.

Children can demonstrate remarkable resilience; however, this trait doesn't negate the fact that a child needs someone to care about them, someone to confide in, and someone to be there whenever needed. Beaten severely once again, Allen retreated to a dark corner of his room and with his purest form of faith as a child, he finally cried out to God for help. His touching plea was answered with a precious gift beyond anyone's imagination.

It's a terrible thing to be all alone with what you can easily call the enemy and there's no escape. There was nowhere to run, and I was uncertain of what tomorrow was going to bring. We were in a prison camp, but I certainly never knew for sure if we were going to survive it. I imagined what death would be like because I didn't know how much more I could take. I laid back and wondered what it would be like to die. Will it hurt? Will I just fall asleep and wake up in another place? Where do I go? Am I just not going to be here anymore? You don't know how strong you are until you must be strong, but my breaking point came after a particularly tough attack.

I was in a dark corner of my room, hurting so bad, and no one was paying any attention to me. I felt the warm trickle of blood down my face, and my eyes were already puffed and swollen shut. I remember being in excruciating pain when I cried out, 'God, I need your help! I need help! God, help me please!' If God could have come down and taken my life at that very moment, I would have appreciated it so much.

I felt a warm presence in that moment as if someone were right there beside me. A comforting warmth radiated and embraced me like a heart-felt hug of pure light, euphoria, and peace. The name Harvey came to mind as if introducing himself to me. I had never met anyone named Harvey in my life before that moment. It's important to mention that at that time we didn't have a television or radio and the movie 'Harvey,' starring Jimmy Stewart, didn't come out in theatres until three years later in 1950.[11] Harvey was very real to me, and I thought, 'Oh my gosh, I have a friend and I am not alone.' It's an awkward thing to explain, but Harvey communicated with me only in my mind and it was very consoling to me to have him to talk to. I spoke to him directly and he answered me in my mind. I can't describe Harvey as more than a radiating warm presence that enveloped me, because there were no facial features, and he didn't have a body. I have never been able to physically touch or see Harvey, only feel his calming and caring presence next to me.

I stayed hidden from my mom as much as possible so I was on my own most of the time and the only person I could get close to was Harvey. I shared with him, and he'd tell me what I needed to hear: 'I love you' and 'You'll be alright' were important responses I needed to hear as a child. Whenever I called out to Harvey, he was right there with me, and I wanted to be there for him too. I cared about him because he cared about me, and I was always afraid that he might get hurt so badly during the beatings that I would lose him. After each beating, I asked, as if he were part of me, which he was, 'Harvey, are you okay?' He always answered, 'Yes, I am okay.' We were often together and if there was ever a time that I called on him and he didn't immediately respond to me, I felt very lost until he did. I loved the fact that I had my very own person who cared so deeply for me and would never abandon me. Knowing that was important and it helped me through my darkest moments.

I remember little Darlene had two imaginary friends, Early and Ramey, and she played with them, but I never played with Harvey. He was only there when I needed his help, but he never needed me in return. I never did anything to help him, but he never expected me to, either. I didn't share Harvey with anyone else, and that was selfish of me, but he was essential for my survival.

Allen and Harvey sitting together in the exact location as they did 75 years ago

My favorite place on the farm to sneak away to and just sit with Harvey was under an oak tree, growing on a bank that overlooked the bend of a freshwater stream. I pried my swollen eyelids open with my fingers to catch a glimpse of the sunlight glancing off the ripples making it shimmer like a million diamonds. It was so incredibly peaceful with just the chirping of nearby birds to be heard. I have people ask me, 'How did you get through this and to whom did you talk with about it? Surely you must have had a psychiatrist.' It's a shame, but I didn't have anyone to talk to about what was happening to me, not even my family members. I was so desperate that I had to manufacture someone in my mind to talk to, but it was all I had. In Harvey, I had someone to be with me, who cared about me, and this made all the difference in the world.

Until now, I never wanted to tell a soul about Harvey for fear people would think I was crazy, and I certainly didn't want a psychiatrist to talk me out of having Harvey. If having him with me makes me crazy, then just leave me this way. I know that when I die, heaven will be filled with angels like Harvey, and it will be a wonderful place to be. My advice to you is this: even if you have to create your own support system to survive, then that's what you must do. You're not giving up, you just found somebody to help you, and that's what I did. I didn't lose my mind, I discovered somebody named Harvey to help me keep it. God didn't take me out of my painful situation that day, but he did provide me with a warrior of the light to help me battle my way through it. I can honestly tell you there is nobody but God who could have known how much I needed Harvey that day, and still do.

Harvey's manifestation was one of Allen's greatest coping strategies and the key to his survival as a child. Fascinated with the concept of Harvey, I couldn't resist digging a little deeper. I discovered that the name Harvey exists in six different alphabets.[12] It is a Christian name with a biblical meaning of "one who is ready for battle, a strong man, a battle-worthy warrior."[13] Harvey is associated with the colors pink and blue and his destiny number is seven. H (8) + A (1) + R (9) + V (4) + E (5) + Y (7) = 34 (3 + 4= 7)[14] Major goosebumps appeared when I realized that Allen was seven when he met Harvey, seven is Harvey's destiny number, I inadvertently wrote about Harvey in chapter seven, and the number seven plays a vital role in the stories and meaning of the Bible being mentioned seven hundred times.[15] An imaginary friend and a figment of a little boy's imagination? Maybe. But the fact that Harvey is still with Allen nearly seventy-seven years later makes me shake my head and smile.

8

When Life Hands You Lemons

*"From every wound there is a scar, and every scar tells a story.
A story that says, 'I survived!'"*
—Quotesgram.com

Life on the Pennsylvania farm was rudimentary at best. The family lived in an uninviting and dilapidated old house with a dank and earthy smell constantly emanating from it. The Dutch Lap was weathered, the siding unpainted, and the metal roof showed signs of aging. Inside, a thin layer of linoleum covering plank wooden floors kept the house frigid throughout the winter. Life was difficult and void of even the most basic of comforts or conveniences. There was no transportation, electricity, heat, or air conditioning, and zero indoor plumbing. Water heated on an antique wooden stove filled the galvanized tub for occasional baths and was shared by more than one person. The foul smelling Fels-Naptha meant to be used for pre-treating stains or as a home remedy for various skin irritants, was their regular bath soap.[16] The only source of heat for the entire house emanated from the kitchen's wood stove which had plates that could be lifted off the top. Without an electric refrigerator in the home, groceries were kept cool by setting them down into a trough filled with flowing waters in a spring house.

In addition, just imagine the back of the farmhouse entirely caved-in with dirt, allowing critters to roam freely inside. In time, there were nearly forty dogs and cats coming and going from the farm depositing messes on the linoleum floor that froze overnight. Every day Allen scrambled at first daylight to scrape it up before his mother found it and threw another fit. Armed with only a BB-gun, Allen tried to kill the venomous copperhead snakes attempting to slither into the house. Unfortunately, he discovered that his toy gun wasn't powerful enough to break the skin, and only made the reptiles move more aggressively.

These deplorable living conditions would have persisted if it weren't for Pop consistently providing groceries, clothing, haircuts, social outings, and money. After a year of living like this, Pop took it upon himself to hire a daily worker to fix the problem. Wheelbarrow by wheelbarrow, the worker removed the dirt and built a solid wall. It was an improvement, but the family still lacked electricity and heat. Coal-oil lamps were lit at night, but once the flame was extinguished, it was ice cold, and no one could see their hand in front of their face. A trek outside to find the outhouse in the woods was a daunting task, so Allen urinated in a bedside can. It was so bitter cold in the house that by morning, the glass of water on the nightstand was frozen solid. Allen shared a bed with his brother which provided much needed body warmth, but sometimes that warmth came from unwanted sources. With all that these boys were going through, it's no wonder Jerry suffered from stress-induced bed-wetting.

I don't know what his problem was, but Jerry peed on me every night and I woke up soaking wet. I felt that and said, 'Jerry, Jerry, you're peeing!' Waking Mom was out of the question, so many times, our bed sheets went unchanged. They either dried out or they didn't, and we just climbed into the same sheets the very next night. Mom would have pummeled Jerry if she ever found out, so we hid this at all costs. In wintertime, the sheets froze, and you could pick them up like sheets of plywood. Jerry remembers wetting the bed until he was thirteen years old and believes it was due to the emotional stress he was under while living at the farm. The bed-wetting eventually stopped, but to this day, I can feel his warm pee on my back.

Without his big brother watching over him, it is seriously doubtful that Jerry would have survived the arduous life on that farm.

Jerry and I were down at the pond where the water flowed underneath the road and came out on the other side forming a stream. There was a big rock that sat close to the road with water flowing underneath it. I heard a splash and Jerry was gone! He was under the water looking up at me with wide eyes and open mouth. The heavy flow of the water pinned him against branches and prevented him from resurfacing. I leaped into the water and tried holding on to the large rock at the same time because I couldn't swim. Slipping off the rock while trying to reach Jerry, I barely got a hold of his wrist and pulled him right up out of the water. He had sucked in a lot of fluid and was coughing and gasping for air. I did my best to always look after my little brother and I knew he would have died without me there that day.

In the kitchen, Jerry came up under one of the open cabinet doors and slammed his head hard. Initially, he shook it off and I thought he was okay until we went to the barn to play. I knew there was something different, but I couldn't put my finger on it. Walking back to the house, Jerry was staggering, and I grabbed his arm. 'What's the matter?' He looked at me with glassy eyes as I kept asking him what was wrong. He was completely unresponsive, so, I took him by the hand back to the house and explained that something was wrong with Jerry. Mom laid him on the couch, and he had no idea where or who he was. Pop was immediately summoned to drive Jerry to the hospital where they kept him under surveillance for a few days healing from a serious concussion.

The naturalist way of life only added to the already stressful and anxiety-laden life that Allen lived. George believed that his therapies were conducted in the best interest of his family, but any sane person would vehemently disagree. However, young Allen trusted George implicitly, never questioning if he told him to drink this or take that. So, when George told him that stripping down naked and walking through the deep snow to stand in an icy pond would keep him from getting a cold, he complied.

Pond Scene – Sketch by Geoffrey Beadle

We did this several times a year, but the first time was a total shock because I had no idea what was going to happen, and Jerry was only two-and-a-half-years-old. The entire family had to undress in the front hallway of our house and leave our clothes behind. We walked out bare naked under the covered porch, down the stairs, and into the deep snow. My feet started to burn because the cold felt like fire at one point. We rushed to the pond about a hundred yards from the house. George broke up the ice with an axe and pushed it aside so we could enter the water. It's strange but being in the water felt warmer than being in the snow. My feet didn't feel as frozen in the mud along the bottom, and we dipped down to our necks for a few minutes at a time. I glanced over at my brother and his lips were blue! We were in the water for only a couple of minutes, but I don't think it was the normal few minutes, because it felt like an eternity. At last, we popped up out of the water and ran back to the house. We were shivering as we gathered around that wood-fired stove in the kitchen for warmth. It took time, but eventually we thawed out. It all seems crazy now, but I don't ever remember catching a cold, so maybe there was something to this crazy and unconventional practice.

Allen wasn't without injury himself. Like any boy on a farm, it wasn't unusual to find ways to hurt himself. What was abnormal was the first aid practices his mother subjected him to. Kitty was thoroughly indoctrinated into the naturalist mentality of healing, avoiding any traditional Western medicinal ways, and risking her son's life.

By the time this happened, Pop had made improvements to the house, paying to have a phone line, furnace, and plumbing installed. I was outside playing and noticed a pigeon walking back and forth on the tin roof of our pig stable. The structure was only five feet high, but the roof was slanted, and I used a pile of wood stacked next to it to climb up and try to catch it. The pigeon didn't fly away so I slowly crawled towards it and at about two feet away, I lunged for it. It flew off and I lost my grip sliding down the slick tin roof and over the edge. There was a rusty nail sticking out and it caught me on my right arm at the elbow. The weight of me falling off the roof and catching that spiked nail ripped my arm clear to the bone. I was able to see the inside of my elbow and I was totally scared. I held my elbow as I ran back to the house. Mom was on the phone with my grandmother talking about the birth of my cousin Janet and when I pulled my hand away to show her what I did, she panicked. For once, she called a doctor, and he arrived within thirty minutes to sew up my gaping wound. Before he could do so, he wanted to give me a Tetanus shot, but Mom stubbornly refused. The experienced doctor explained how I might come down with Tetanus or Lockjaw and may even die without the shot, but she held her ground. In good conscience he couldn't sew up my gaping wound without the shot, so he packed his medical instruments back into his bag and headed for the door. I do remember him looking back at me solemnly and shaking his head in disbelief. I knew then that I was going to die.

Mom called out back of the house to two men working on the tractor. They came in to help as she began cutting up eight to ten lemons and squeezing the fresh juice into a container. The two men lifted me up on the table and I was totally scared because the whole experience felt bad. She instructed the men to hold my arm in such a way that the cut was wide open and facing her. She poured that lemon juice into my deep cut. I thought my arm was being cut off because there was so much pain. It was a pain I never felt before in my life, and I was feeling every drop of that juice-screaming and writhing in pain. When she finished, she used a metal fork to dive into the flesh and extract the lemon seeds, one-by one. Finally, she dried off my arm and wrapped adhesive tape around it to close the wound which took an exceptionally long time to heal completely.

*It always oozed with puss, and she'd have me lay out in the sun
and allow the flies to land on it which she swore would help. To
this day, there are two scars that I carry. One is a long scar on
my right elbow because the wound was never closed properly,
and the other is on my mind from the entire insane experience.*

George read *Black Beauty* to Allen each night before bedtime,
but how could such an "angelic man" force his family into an icy
pond the very next day? Why was he so resolute about his naturalist
treatments and yet so weak when it came to standing up to being
slapped, punched, and kicked by his wife? A silent man consents.[17]
George's silence lent consent to the way Kitty treated him, and it also
made him complicit in her treatment of the children. He may as well
have been abusing the boys himself when he didn't stop his wife from
brutalizing her children, but he was weak, complacent, and broken
too. This fact became agonizingly evident when Kitty, who was having
sex with the various workers her father was sending to the house, was
brazen enough to do so right upstairs while George and the boys were
home.

*Mom's middle sister, Doris, was married to Jerry Evans. He was
a boxer in the Army and my brother Jerry is named in his honor.
I used to lay in bed and fantasize that if anything happened to
my mom, I would like to have them as my parents. I used to love
learning how to box from my Uncle Jerry. He taught me how to
keep moving my feet while staying ready to strike. He pointed
out the importance of watching my opponents' eyes for their next
move and I felt empowered by his lessons. He was so tough and
not afraid to fight anyone. I recall when I was nine years old,
Uncle Jerry drove up to the farmhouse and I ran to him and
said, 'We're having a problem here, Uncle Jerry.' He asked,
'What's the matter? What's going on here?' Pushing me aside,*

he burst into the house to find George sitting there crying. Uncle Jerry asked George, 'Why are you crying?' George couldn't say a thing and simply pointed upstairs. Mom was upstairs having sex with another man and all this meek man could do was cry about it. Uncle Jerry leaped up the stairs, crashed through the door, and pulled the man off. He beat him to within one inch of his life, sending him tumbling in his own blood down the stairs. I thought for sure that Uncle Jerry was going to kill that man. He lifted him up by his throat and shoved him out of the house! Pop had to be aware of his daughter's sexual promiscuity, but he didn't have the stones to make her stop. He was afraid that if we were taken away again, he and Nana would have to raise us. Nana certainly didn't want us and so he was caught in the middle of it all.

Nobody, not even Pop, would make his daughter stop her detestable behavior. More than likely, it was out of guilt that he provided everything she and the family needed.

She took advantage of Pop by giving him long grocery lists and he did all the shopping and personally delivered it to the farm. He filled his large Hudson with groceries for us and then she handed him telephone bills for long-distance calls to a naturalist doctor in California. Pop was visibly upset and argued with her because the costly phone bills were ridiculous and unnecessary. Pop put Mom in such a dreadful mood that afterwards I had to do everything in my power to bring her back down from the dangerous levels of anger she felt. To survive, I learned to appease her and make sure I didn't get blamed for any of it, which was almost impossible to do.

I hated the fact that she played socialite using all Pop's groceries to feed her friends and neighbors instead of us. The chocolate milk, ice cream, or whatever was all hers to enjoy and we were never allowed to take anything out of the refrigerator. Sometimes she even drank the milk right in front of us and it was torturous. This is the reason today, it is the biggest compliment for me to tell my guests, 'Please, help yourself! Anything in the refrigerator is yours to enjoy.'

Looking back, Mom was sick and should never have been allowed to have children. There were many days where I wished I had never been born and wanted more than anything to have that day taken back.

9
Bubblegum Rebellion

"Breathe darling. This is just a chapter, not your whole story."
–SC Lourie

When Allen moved to the farm, he attended the second grade just a mile up the road, in a primitive one-room country schoolhouse. In the center of the room stood a boiler stove which was fed wood throughout the day to fuel the flames, keeping the class feeling toasty. Twenty students of every educational level from first to eighth grade, occupied the same room. The teacher must have been a differentiated instructional champion to manage the learning taking place. There was no electricity and no other facilities such as a cafeteria, gymnasium, or library. A simple and rarely cleaned outhouse was placed behind the schoolhouse for all to share.

Ms. Hammershe's one-room school house
uphill from the PA farm

Ms. Hamershee was unforgivingly strict and terribly stern with the children in her class. I suppose she had to be mean to manage any classroom management issues with teenage boys and six-year-olds all crammed into the same space. Ms. Hamershee was feared for her tendency to whack her students on the back three times with the long handle of her oak chalkboard pointer-especially if they were tardy. Walking uphill to school in all types of weather, there were times when Allen realized he wouldn't arrive in time and just turned around and walked back home rather than face the sting of that pointer. Kitty wasn't the least bit interested in sending Allen to school anyway, so she never looked up when he returned. Nor did she ever inquire about his school day, proudly display any projects on the refrigerator door, help with homework, or take the time to read progress reports. At best she managed to pack a daily lunch, albeit with some grossly unappetizing sandwiches.

The sandwiches she packed were disgusting, like endive and carrot sandwiches she made for me to carry to school. Watercress is hot and sometimes I ate watercress, raisin, and carrot sandwiches or just a slice of raw onion between two pieces of bread slathered with mayonnaise. When I was able to go to school, we ate lunch at our desks and the other kids watched me eating this stuff and were interested as heck. 'What are you eating?' I told them what it was and out of curiosity, they all wanted to try it. I'd strike a deal telling them that I'd trade them my whole sandwich for just half of theirs.

Allen consistently missed school, but rarely for more than three consecutive days at a time, which required a signed doctor's note. Kitty wrote notes to Ms. Hammershee with every excuse under the sun.

I rarely went to school more than three days a week and Mom produced all kinds of excuses for me. I had diarrhea, a cold, sore throat, or headache, and she overused these excuses repeatedly. 'Mom, you used diarrhea last time!' It was ridiculous. I remember Ms. Hammershee exclaimed, in front of the whole class, 'You know what? If you were sick as much as you are absent, you would've been dead long ago!' Of course, everyone erupted in a roar of laughter. I felt so ashamed because there was truly nothing wrong with me. I was healthy as a horse and the teacher knew that too, but not once did she mention anything about my swollen eyes and face, or the dark bruises on my arms. When other kids noticed and spoke up, I was quick with a story of what happened to me. It was crucial to be very convincing because I couldn't take the chance that anyone would contact my mom about it. I made certain everyone at school understood: 'Yes, I fell down the steps yesterday and, whew boy, look what happened.'

"Summertime" Circa 1948

I convinced them that it wasn't my mom because in the end, nobody was going to take me out of my home and far away from her. If I could have been guaranteed that somebody would take me out of there, I would have thrown her under the bus in a heartbeat. The sad reality was that nobody seemed to care enough about me to investigate the situation. Back then, it was all about the parents. It was their rules, and you could bet that they always ruled the roost.

Allen missed the third grade altogether because Kitty exhausted her list of excuses. She was afraid that Allen would tell someone or eventually questions would be raised, so keeping him away from others was in her best interest. When Allen didn't come back to school, the administration sent the truant officer to the farmhouse. Based upon what Kitty told the officer and the erratic behavior he witnessed first-hand from Allen, he was convinced that this child wasn't fit to attend school.

I had to act like a crazy person when the truant officer came to the house to investigate why I was missing every day of my third-grade year. Mom demanded I run up and down the stairs and around the house screaming and carrying on wildly the entire time the officer was there. I was out of control! God knows in my childhood I witnessed more than my share of examples of someone acting crazy, so as you can imagine, I was very convincing. The truant officer witnessed all of this and agreed that I wasn't fit to attend school. He never did return to the farm, and I never returned to that school.

The only consistent thing in Allen's young life was his mother's fits of rage and the regular beatings he endured. He and Jerry were pushed and pulled into various situations and always uprooted for one reason or another. Infidelity, hardships, and abusive rages took its toll on Kitty's marriage to George and at one time she even uprooted the boys for six months to move in with a family friend in

Schuylkill Haven. When that situation failed too, she moved back in with George and Pop Jones on the farm, but the lack of stability was in and of itself abusive. At times I find it so hard to believe that I am writing about Allen's mother. The term mother means to bring up, care for, provide for, and to look after someone kindly and protectively.[18] At best, Kitty was nothing more than a biological sponsor and never worthy of being called Mother. Aware of his daughter's deficiencies, Pop did everything he could to provide food, clothing, shelter, and the tools needed to become more self-sufficient.

We couldn't grow our own food even though Pop bought everything we needed. George hinted to Pop that if he had a tractor and all the necessary implements to go along with it, we could plant crops and support ourselves. That was a laughable statement, but Pop spent thousands of dollars on a brand-new Ford tractor and implements. The minute they unloaded it off the truck, George climbed up into the seat sending my mom into this hissy fit. She continued as if he was going to die if he moved the tractor even an inch. She commanded him to get off that tractor, and did you know, that man never got back on it. A brand-new tractor!

A nearby neighbor, Martin Strayer was a mean drunk, but he was a good farmer. He grew a variety of produce and dairy products enough to sell to the surrounding community. Allen was sent walking over to his farm to buy milk and butter on a regular basis. Ms. Strayer was a diligent woman. She never sat down to rest and worked her fingers to the bone, mucking stalls, feeding livestock, milking cows, churning butter, and keeping the house. She always wore an old, faded house dress with stockings rolled halfway up to her knees and her gray-hair pulled back into a bun. She was kind and friendly to Allen, but her husband was a different story.

Mom sent me over to the Strayer's farm one day to buy freshly churned butter. I was standing inside the house while Ms. Strayer was measuring out the butter, spoon by spoon onto a scale. With exactly a pound of butter, she folded it into wax paper and twisted the ends shut so I could carry it home.

As she was twisting the ends shut, Mr. Strayer came staggering in drunk and yelling at me, 'What the hell are you doing here boy?' I was shocked because I always thought he and I were friends. He never once said a cross word to me before this. 'Just leave him alone Martin, he's getting butter.' 'Like hell he is!' Mr. Strayer caught a hold of me and started smacking me and when I fell to the floor, he began kicking me. Throwing her arms around his neck, Ms. Strayer leaped on his back and pulled him over on top of her. She kept hollering, 'Run, Allen! Run!' I ran all the way back home and my mom took one look at me and asked, 'What happened to you?' I told her how our neighbor beat me up and she said, 'Well, where's the butter?' 'I am sorry, Mom! I had to leave without it.'

Just two weeks after that incident I was back over there buying from Ms. Strayer. She warned me to make sure my favorite dog, Queenie, didn't come down to their farm again because Martin threatened to kill her if she did. While walking to school a couple of days later, I came across my beloved dog, Queenie lying along the side of the road. As promised, Martin shot her with his shotgun. Poor girl tried to make it home and got as far as she could before collapsing. Instead of going on to school, I carefully picked her up in my arms and carried her back to the farm and buried her. That was one mean man that would kill a boy's best friend.

Kitty took everything of value from her boys. If they made a dollar, she was the first one to take it away and use it for herself. This happened every single time the boys were given a dollar and Allen was becoming tired of it. In an act of rebellion, Allen took off for the local country store the minute that dollar hit his hand.

All summer long, I went without shoes or shirt. With just shorts on, my skin turned copper brown from the sun. One day a couple of men stopped at the neighbor's house about a quarter mile down the road. They were asking about the best places to go hunting in our area. The neighbors pointed them our way because Mom didn't care either way and George had no say in it. These hunters took one look at me and said, 'Wow, you're like a little Indian boy! We'll give you a dollar if you can lead us to a field where we can hunt pheasants or rabbits.' I knew the farm like the back of my hand, having explored every inch of it, so for a dollar I led them to all the best hunting spots.

"Copper Brown"
Allen and Jerry Circa 1950

When they left, Mom immediately asked me if they gave me anything to help them. I confessed, 'Yeah, they gave me a dollar,' and she immediately took it from me. Pop used to give us each a dollar when he came to cut our hair and she always took that as well. When I got a little older and Pop gave me a dollar, I'd run and get on my bicycle and ride over the hill about three miles to a little country store. With my dollar I bought twenty pieces of Bazooka bubblegum. It was a penny for a little square of gum and I would buy twenty of them. I returned home and Mom would ask, 'Well, where's your dollar?' I explained how I used some of it to buy bubblegum, and I knew she would get terribly upset with me, but I wanted to get something for my dollar. I gave her the eighty cents in change, but I was done with earning a dollar for this and that and never getting to spend any of it. Disappointed, Jerry would say to me, 'Why didn't you take my dollar too, and get me twenty pieces of gum?' He was the one that totally lost out, but I did share my gum with him that day.

Like the boys, George had been through a lot of pain and abuse at the hands of his wife. She broke her second husband's heart and spirit on more than one occasion, and at the age of forty-four his health was declining. George was diagnosed with Dropsy which is an older medical term for Edema. More than likely, it was the onset of congestive heart failure causing both of his legs to swell, making it painful and challenging to walk. A man that poured his heart and soul into trying to heal his abusive, unfaithful, and loafing wife for years, was now dependent upon her actions to save his life.

George died when I was ten years old. It was December 29, 1950, while we were visiting my mom's youngest sister, Jeanette, and her husband Cecil. George suffered from Dropsy which caused his legs to swell up with fluid and he had a challenging time maintaining his balance. As we were leaving the house late that night, George tripped and hit his head on the hot water radiator and knocked himself out. My Uncle Cecil dragged George over and laid him on the floor in front of the sofa. Mom immediately got on the phone trying to reach this naturalist doctor in California, but he didn't answer. My aunt and uncle started getting worried about George who was laying flat out on their floor still unconscious yet breathing.

Finally, they made the decision to call a local doctor to the house. Not long after the call, Dr. Bartley came in and immediately kneeled next to George to listen with his stethoscope. Mom went absolutely insane yelling at the doctor, 'Don't you touch him! Don't you touch him! I am his wife, and I am telling you, do not touch him!' Reluctantly, Dr. Bartley backed off and we could see George's chest rising and falling with each breath. Mom tried again to reach her naturalist doctor, but it was no use, he still wasn't answering the phone. I remember my cousin Janet was crying in her crib in the other room. All the commotion woke her up, and I felt bad for my aunt who had to keep trying to soothe her. It was a traumatizing sight to see my fat mother leaning over George's lifeless body screaming at him, 'Wake up, George! Get up! Get up!' Several hours passed and finally, Mom said, 'Okay! See what you can do.' Dr. Bartley placed the stethoscope on George's chest and said, 'I am sorry, but this man is gone.' Mom was in total shock, crying out, 'Oh no! Oh no! No!'

We were there all night and we all watched George Jones die in front of us with a medical doctor sitting right there being told not to touch him. It's a shame because I don't think George had to die that night. If an ambulance had been called, he would have lived. All she needed to do was to let go of her control over everything. She had to control everyone and everything and it caused that man's death. Pop Jones was a hard man and never shed a tear, but when the news hit the farm, I could tell that his heart was broken. He just wanted to know if his son said anything before he died. Unfortunately, George never regained consciousness that night, and would never get the chance to give us one last message to tell his father, 'I love you.'

10

Greenhorn

"God is in control, but he doesn't expect you to lean on a shovel and pray for a hole."
–Stan Terry

Kitty was a fanatic about always needing people around her and she constantly attracted different people to her. Men or women-it didn't matter, her fear of being alone kept her constantly craving attention. She was always the life of every gathering with her gregarious personality, but could be crude in her comments, especially while in the company of other women. She frequently used the phrase in jest, 'Up your Giggy with a wire brush!' Everyone within earshot would laugh aloud, even if it were out of pure astonishment at the vulgarity she so comfortably used. Grotesquely overweight, Kitty was not an attractive woman and yet she could draw men to herself like moths to a flame with her boisterous and promiscuous behavior. In her carelessness and total disregard for the well-being of her children, Kitty had sex with men in communal areas of the house where it was all too easy for Allen or Jerry to accidentally walk in on the act.

> *After George died, I spent the next four years being hit and beaten by her and watching her have several men come and go. She didn't know I walked in on her, but I looked up and saw her on the sofa having sex. It made me sick. It was a troubled time because I saw things that a ten-year-old boy shouldn't have seen.*

I immediately looked away, but you can't unsee something like that. It really bothered me, but at that time, I was trapped. I was there and there was no getting away from it all.

It wasn't long after George died that Kitty pulled the boys off the farm again. They went to live with Chris Johnson and his family in the small town of Cressona, which was less than five miles from Pottsville. The awkwardness of this situation was found in the fact that Chris had been coming to the farm to work on the tractor and have sex with Kitty long before George died. Now, he was having the affair with her right there in his own home under the nose of his sweet wife who gave him two children of their own. For obvious reasons, this shared living arrangement didn't last long. Once again, Allen was uprooted from school, flunking out of the sixth grade altogether. Back on the farm, Allen learned how to run that Ford tractor and kept busy working day and night in the fields. At the early age of ten, Allen found that working and staying busy was essential to surviving. This hard work became another coping mechanism that would allow him to plow through the roughest times imaginable.

When I was ten, one of the men that my mom was having sexual relations with took the time to show me how to run the tractor, and I did it. I plowed the fields and planted a hundred acres of corn, wheat, and beans. Other farmers would come in and harvest the crops when they were ready, and although we earned some money from that, it wasn't enough to keep us going. I am positive that Pop wondered why, with a new tractor decked out with all the implements, we still couldn't grow our own food to support ourselves.

Riding that tractor in the fields, I can remember two remarkably close calls. The tractor had an implement called a Spring Tooth Harrow attached to it. The Harrow had at least one hundred curved metal teeth designed to break up the sod, leaving the field dirt soft and smooth. One day while plowing the fields, I managed to catch it on an underground tree root. Much to my horror, the front end of the tractor raised straight up into the air, and I was left hanging onto the steering wheel with both hands. I had no way of getting off safely at that point, so I just held on the best that I could. If that tractor had continued upwards any father, it would have gone over backwards crushing me underneath it. To my amazement, the tractor ran out of gas and stalled just at the tipping point, and the front end lowered back down slowly to the ground. I was in total shock thinking that if I had filled the gas tank that morning, I might have been killed that afternoon.

Another brush with death came when I was ploughing on the side of the hill. It wasn't a particularly steep hill, but I noticed this large rock ahead of me and thought, 'I'll just straddle that.' Just as I was approaching the rock, the tractor slid a little bit sending the uphill tire directly over the rock where it got caught up. Without me steering, the wheels turned abruptly on their own, sending us down the hill perfectly fine. I was shaking on the tractor seat. Someone was looking out for me, but it was certainly not my mom. I thought it was ironic that she came unglued if her husband George even sat on the tractor for one minute, but she didn't think twice about a ten-year-old getting on it and disappearing out of sight for most of the day.

Two years after George was laid to rest, Kitty began communicating back and forth with Larry Nelson who was living in California. More than likely, he was a connection made through the naturalist doctor Kitty talked with regularly. She painted a pretty picture in her correspondence with Larry telling him that as a widow, she owned this working farm in Pennsylvania and was searching for companionship.

Lucy was Kitty's friend living in Reading who was encouraging the relationship, offering her home as a place where they could meet one another in person.

After George died, Mom remarried a man named Larry Nelson whom she had met in some newspaper ad-or some kind of lonely-hearts' club back then. He lived in California, but they communicated on the phone and in letters. Lo and behold, the next thing I knew, he showed up at our farm. Mom had a friend who lived in Reading, Pennsylvania and Larry and she would get together at her house, and the friend was happy about all of this. I don't know if she was the matchmaker or whatever, but she was in favor of them getting married. The next thing I know they are getting married and this friend of my mom's and some- one else attended the wedding and Jerry and I were just standing there not knowing what to think.

After attending the wedding, we drove the hour and half back to the farm. Larry was disappointed in the place and was expecting it to be so much more than it was. The farm really was in terrible shape and very run down at that time. He changed his attitude after that, and he and my mother started arguing with each other. I wanted to step away from all the yelling, so I went outside to play with one of our many dogs. I was calling my mom's third husband, Larry and he got me aside and told me, 'Okay, I am your father now. I want you to call me Dad or Daddy. Don't call me Larry anymore, okay?' So, I called him Dad, but I didn't like it at all because I couldn't stand him from the minute, I met him. He was very fake, arrogant, and not at all down-to-earth. To think he was now going to be my stepfather, oh my gosh, I was so disturbed and on edge about the whole thing. I still had memories of my real dad. I know George did the best he could, but Larry seemed like he came from a different world, and I couldn't relate to him whatsoever. Plus, he never paid any attention to me, or Jerry, and we couldn't stand the guy.

After about three weeks, I woke up to this noise and it was just getting dawn. I looked out the window and saw Larry getting into his car, driving down the road, and thankfully, that was the last we ever saw of him. About a week later we got word that he was back in California and my grandfather had the marriage annulled based on the fib that the marriage was never consummated. Pop still had connections in the judicial system, so he could easily make the whole situation disappear.

Although Allen took on adult level farm chores, he was still just a kid at heart and a greenhorn when it came to interacting with girls.

I am not sure of the family connection with Mom, but when I was a teenager, a couple visited the farm with their two young daughters. One of them was a beautiful sixteen-year-old girl named Mary Lee whom I will never forget. She and her younger sister were playing Hide-and-Seek with me and Jerry around the farm. Me and Mary Lee teamed up and were hiding together in the hayloft of the barn. We were laying there in the hay and I was peering through one of the cracks between the boards, on the lookout for Jerry and her little sister. The next thing I know, Mary Lee put her arm around me to snuggle. She began blowing on my neck and tried to kiss me. She was making all kinds of noise and I said, 'What are you doing? Be quiet! They're going to find us!' I kept looking intently through the floorboards and she tried kissing me again, and I exclaimed, 'Mary Lee, stop!' I didn't understand what she was trying to do, and my biggest concern was losing the game. I was so embarrassed, and thank God, I never ran into her again where she'd say, 'Do you remember

that time in the hayloft when you didn't know what to do?' Sigh.
Yes, well, I didn't know what to do. Puberty was happening to
me, but I was such a Greenhorn. Mostly because I had never
been on a date or gone with any girl because my mom was so
controlling. It was sick, but she always made me tell others that
she was the only woman I would ever want. Mom made me
insist in front of others that I was never going to date anyone, and
I certainly was never going to marry. Looking back, I recognize
that she was grooming me from the onset of puberty to be much
more to her than a son.

View from the PA farmhouse across the pond to the old barn (2022)

Allen did everything he could, but the one hundred acres of crops
didn't bring in enough money to keep the entire place going. The
farm was surrendered for just sixty-five-hundred-dollars in back
taxes owed. After four years of sinking thousands of dollars into what
seemed like a bottomless money pit, and disgusted with his daughter's
inability to help herself, Pop let it all go back to the bank. He moved
Kitty and the boys back home to Pottsville, but sadly, it was Pop Jones
who utterly lost everything. He moved out of the country to Schuylkill

Haven town where he died in 1956 at the age of seventy-seven. Allen and Jerry would never see Pop Jones again once they vacated the farm for the very last time.

Allen standing in front of the PA farmhouse in 2022

11

Morally Bankrupt

"I can be changed by what happens to me,
but I refuse to be reduced by it."
—Maya Angelou

Pop owned a three-story apartment building in Pottsville at 1215 West Market Street. On the street level of this recently renovated building was a beauty parlor and right behind that, was an office Pop used for his work with the Hoover Company. Just off the street, there was a short flight of stairs used to access the first-floor apartment where Allen, Jerry, and Kitty moved into. They had a small patio overlooking the main street and, in the apartment above them, Pop and Nana were in residence. Both apartments looked out, directly across the street, at Patterson Junior High School where Allen enrolled in the sixth grade. Jerry never attended school while living on the farm, so he was just now starting in the first grade at Garfield Elementary. Kitty continued to control every aspect of Allen and Jerry's lives only letting them attend school intermittently. As Jerry described it, these were some of the toughest times imaginable.

Jerry reflects:

> *Some of the single hardest times were when we didn't get to go to school on a regular basis. One of us had to stay home with mother while the other one went to school. I went Monday and Allen went Tuesday. I'd stay home Tuesday and then Wednesday came, and I'd say, 'Allen I have a big test today.' He said, 'Well, so do I.' We argued about this, but one of us ended up having to*

Hershey Park with Jerry, and
cousins Janet and Robert Circa 1953

*stay home. The school year was one hundred and eighty days
and we went maybe ninety days total. It was difficult for us to
keep up with the other students, but Mom didn't care about that.
Considering I was rarely in class, it was amazing that I never
flunked anything. I was so proud of my grades, but she never
cared to look over my report card. There were times when she
called the school, 'Please send Jerry home, right away!' This was
the day I was able to go to my classes and now, I have to come
back! Mom told me she just felt like I needed to be there with her.*

Allen felt the same way.

*In school I didn't attend dances or play sports because I always
had to be home right after school. I was President of the sketch
club, and although it was a hobby, I don't think I did very well.
I pulled from objects in my mind like a plane, and sketched just*

the wing and the engine, and you'd see just that part of the plane and not the whole object. I liked the concept of seeing part of something and making it obvious what it was in a sketch. Maybe it was because people couldn't see the whole picture of what was happening to me as a child. They just saw bits and pieces, but it should have been obvious from those pieces what the whole picture of my life looked like.

Fear holds a tremendous amount of power in it, even more so than love. Allen and Jerry absolutely feared their mom and as a result, she used it to exercise complete control over them. She micromanaged every aspect of their lives, determining who they spent time with, spoke to, and what was said. In Pottsville, Allen and Jerry were around more people than they were when tucked away on the farm. With more social interaction came the realization that this situation with their mother wasn't even close to being normal. Kitty ruled their entire social lives and became overly jealous especially if they showed any interest in girls.

1215 West Market Street in Pottsville, PA

Jerry remembers this control:

I was just incredibly happy whenever somebody paid attention to me, especially Peggy who was a delightful young lady who walked home from school with me. Thinking back, she must have had an inner sense that something wasn't right with this boy, but I like him very much. She had to have known, but unfortunately, I couldn't like her very much because of Mom. We'd be walking down the street and Mom would be hanging over the railing watching us the entire time which was extremely intimidating. Peggy lived on the same side of the street as me and not that far away, but I had to walk directly to our apartment, go inside, and not come back out until it was time to go to school. When anyone showed an interest in being friendly or conversing, I'd really latch on to it and wish we could do more together.

I never mentioned my home life to other kids. I never asked, 'Do you get to go to movies or go to parties?' I never asked because I already knew the answer. 'Of course! Why? Don't you?' It wouldn't have done me any good, so I had no social life whatsoever until I was nineteen or twenty years old. The only association was to sit next to somebody in class or at lunch and talk to them. It's a wonder I could communicate at all. I mean, I wasn't a social misfit to the point where nobody wanted to be around me, but, I had enough left in the tank to say a few things to people. Other kids had parents who cared about them, taught them things, and took them places. They experienced things, but we never did. I couldn't have friends. I couldn't go out at night or on the weekends. I couldn't do anything with any of my school friends or neighbors, but Mom and Nana certainly did. They dragged us to three or four different homes to visit with some of their long-time friends. Mom wanted to get out of the house and

*have people see her and for her to see somebody, but she could
care less if we had any friends.*

*I realized this wasn't normal when I reached junior high and
people commented, 'You need to join the band, or you need to
play basketball and football. Why don't you come out and try
out for this or that?' We never could! We never had card games
or anything like that to play with at home. It was so incredibly
difficult. We couldn't even stay overnight with our aunts and
uncles or socialize with our own cousins. Nah, Mom was always
afraid we'd speak out to the point where we may convince somebody, in whatever household we were able to visit, that we were
in an extremely dangerous situation.*

*Even if it were only black and white, if it weren't for television,
I think we would have shot ourselves. If we had found a way to
do it, we would have. All the time we were growing up Mom
insisted, 'You can have all the girlfriends you want, but there's
no one in this world who is going to be any better than your
mother. No one will be as loyal and faithful to you as your own
mother.'*

Kitty only cared about herself and functioned as if she was the
most important person in the world. Everyone else simply existed to
cater to her every wish, especially her children. Jerry explains:

*It's like we did something barely wrong, and we were put away
for life because of it. We thought, 'This can't be normal.'
Eventually we did realize that this is not normal. I know it is
incredibly hard to understand, but she never cared about us in
any way, except for what we could give her. What she wanted
was a warm body to be in the same room with her, so that she
was never alone. She could care less about us as people, only as
things. As someone there to keep her company and satisfy her*

every need. Allen and I took care of a lot of her needs. She never asked us, but always demanded, 'Get up and get me this or that! Give me the phone and give me a box of crackers!' She was so fat that getting up and getting out of the chair was incredibly laborious. We had to grab her by the arms and pull her out of her chair. I mean she was huge, yelling, 'You need to do my hair!' So, we would have to rub her head and stand behind her and if we didn't do it the way she wanted it done, she'd turn around and give us a slap. 'My feet hurt! You gotta rub my feet!' Then oh my God, we had to do her feet. If we didn't, she kicked us either in the chest or face. 'Get up and do it right!'

There are so many things you hate to say about your mother, but one thing I know is that she was incredibly selfish. There's no question in my mind that all she ever thought about was herself. Whatever she could achieve through us was her main ambition. She was shockingly hateful and took away everything we had. Allen chimes in:

She got one of us out of bed to brush her hair, rub her head or back, and massage her feet. We did this sometimes until one or two o'clock in the morning or however long it took for her to feel like she could doze off. When she saw me drift to sleep while rubbing her feet, she kicked me, and I mumbled, 'I'm awake, I'm awake!' I was so exhausted and could hardly stay awake to do this, but that didn't matter to her. I wasn't anything she cared about, and I just needed to do whatever it took to bring her pleasure.

Trying to do whatever it took to appease his mother and prevent her from blowing up, Allen followed her from room to room. Kitty's response to this would haunt her son for the rest of his life.

Slamming doors, oh my gosh, slamming doors. I had to follow her in one room and out the other. She would slam the door in

my face and expect me to follow her. I followed her and she
would slam another door in my face and on and on this went.
To this day, if you get upset with me, don't go into a room,
and slam the door because I will never come through that
door after you.

Kitty was a pro at manipulation and found pleasure in making
her boys feel guilty and regret the fact that they were ever born. Being
born to her was a debt to be paid with every aspect of their lives. Jerry
recalls:

She was on the phone constantly with a naturalist doctor in
California, discussing her nervous condition. Allegedly she had
a couple of nervous breakdowns and that was the reason for the
way she was. She reminded us constantly, 'You know, I don't
really want to be this way.' I can remember it like it was yester-
day. 'I don't want to be this way, but you know, I was in labor
with you for forty-eight hours and almost died giving birth to
you, so you need to be thankful. The reason I am the way I am
is because of giving birth to you.' You know, there was more than
once when we'd go to leave the apartment in a taxicab to visit
her friends or something, and I thought, 'What if I gave her a
little nudge and pushed her down the steps?' She was so big that
she could have easily lost her footing, and nobody would have
ever known any difference, but I never did. I never did and
that's a horrible thing to even think about, but I thought
about it because I could only handle so much. My mental and
physical state were beyond frazzled.

In her demented and sick ways, Kitty was a mother that had to be
pleased, who used outrage, physical violence, and fear to control her
children along with guilt and shame to demoralize them. Kitty
trained Allen his entire life to the point that saying no to anything

she did was no longer an option. She was a textbook sociopath and a psychopath that fits the description of a predator to a "T": Lacks empathy, manipulative, feels entitled, controls everything, great at lying, deceptive, ridicules, isolates her victim from friends and family, intimidating, narcissistic, finds excuses for their actions, seems perfect at first, adjusts their behavior with different people, need I write more?[19] Allen was groomed from the day he was born, abused in every way imaginable, until the unimaginable happened. Kitty's routine incestual rape of her son proved beyond any doubt that she was morally bankrupt.

Allen Circa 1953   Laura Darlene Williams   Jerry Sterner

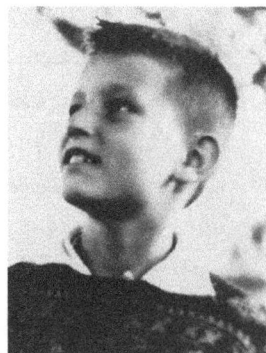

It was in essence the very worst beating I could've ever gotten. I would have rather she hit me. She finally produced the ultimate beating and the ultimate disgrace. I don't know why she wanted to humiliate me so badly and make me feel like I wasn't worthy, and I didn't count. I thought, 'How could a mother, after everything she put me through, be proud of her son?' She never stopped trying to tear me down or dehumanize me. Years of beatings I could heal from and not feel pain anymore, but the sexual things my mother did to me were as if she hung me like Jesus on the cross. It's a pain in my heart that I will have until the

day I die. I can never erase what she made me do starting when I was in sixth grade and continuing until I was a sophomore in high school.

Mom needed me to come to her room where she slept in this twin bed. It was too tight of a spot, especially sharing with a person who weighed over three hundred pounds. She wanted me to face her, but I turned my back to her, and she finally agreed to that. We had no conversation about it at all. She just came to my room and wanted me to follow her back to her room. I knew what it was all about because it happened quite often. It started out with her holding me close to her while she used the cut off end of a broom handle to satisfy herself. I knew what she was doing as she held me closer, closer, tighter, and tighter. I thought, 'Oh my God, just let it be over! Please let it be over!' Other times, she fondled me and forced me tight against her rolls of fat until she was exhausted with sexual gratification. It was disgusting and my mind simply detached. I had to have a place in my mind where I could go, separate from my body and what was happening to me physically. Harvey was never present with me during the sexual abuse because I purposely shut him out. There was nothing he could do to console me during something so heinous. I guess I didn't want Harvey to see it because I felt so ashamed.

Once it was all over, Mom finally released me to go back to my bed. I had the hardest time getting back to sleep because I felt like I had done something terribly wrong. I hated the fact that I was part of that, and I constantly felt dirty. I thought to myself, 'How can anybody do that to somebody they love? A child? A son?' I felt very used and very dirty, and it was a terrible time in my life. When I went to school, I felt like some-how, someway, people were able to see it. As if it was all around me as some kind of visual thing because I felt it so strongly and I was incredibly embarrassed. In all my childhood of being terrorized, the way I was used as a sexual object by my mom is what I hated the most.

Allen had to find a way to survive and move beyond his internal and external pain, and the only way he knew how to do this was by staying mentally untouchable. Barely in his teens, Allen realized that when his mind was stronger than his emotions, he could live through anything. There was no one he could talk to about the incestual rape happening to him at the hands of his own mother. This was one secret he desperately had to hide for the last seventy years. Who could even remotely understand the mental and physical anguish he endured at the hands of the one person who was supposed to love and protect?

12

Music to My Ears

"The caged bird sings with a fearful trill of things unknown
but longed for still and his tune is heard on the distant hill
for the caged bird sings of freedom"
–Maya Angelou from, 'I Know Why the Caged Bird Sings.'

Kitty argued with her mother daily, exchanging obscenities with the foulest of language that even the most hardened of sailors would blush at. Jerry recollects:

It was a horrible relationship between my mother and Nana. There was slamming of doors, yelling, throwing things, and cussing. They didn't get along at all, and it was terrible to watch. Mom was just like Nana in so many ways. You would think that if Mom treated us this way, we could get some love and support from Nana. No! Not whatsoever, because she didn't really care for us either.

Kitty was a very insecure person who couldn't stand to be alone and always needed someone to be with her. She was so codependent, wanting her mother to constantly come downstairs and stay with her, but Nana preferred getting away from her daughter and the house, paying friends a visit, or shopping downtown for new clothes. Her favorite pass-time was sitting next to her best friend on a bench in the heart of downtown Pottsville, just people watching. They loved to gawk as people walked by, laugh, whisper and pass judgement. The bickering between the mother daughter duo escalated to a point that Nana couldn't stand it any longer and demanded Pop buy her a different house. As with every other insistence, Pop complied and bought the house just two doors down, at 1211 West Market Street.

Nana was mean-spirited and constantly found fault in her husband which she loudly vocalized every day. Jerry explains:

Pop and Nana never had a loving relationship. They never said a kind word to each other in all the years they were married. Once or twice in the summer, we drove to Hershey Park, which was a highlight. Pop drove while Nana sat behind him quarreling the entire way to and from the park. Nana banged on the back of Pop's seat and hit his headrest with her fist. Totally frustrated with her behavior, Pop threw his hands up in the air with animated Italian gestures and barked back at her.

Pop worked hard, but it was his work which kept him out of the line of fire of the one woman that lived to make his life miserable. Music recharged his spirit and helped to keep him overall jovial and positive. He adored music and wanted his grandson to be exposed to it, so he bought Allen his first guitar. With any spare time, Pop spent time teaching Allen how to play guitar and accompany him while playing his mandolin. Those precious few memories bonding with his grandfather, would mean more to Allen than anything money could ever buy. That one secondhand gift was the catalyst for the changes Allen so desperately needed in his life. Music became one of Allen's most important coping mechanisms and swung wide the doors to new opportunities and friends. Allen now held in his hands the tool to build self-confidence which guided him to freedom from his battered and sheltered existence. Little did Pop realize that his thoughtful gift would save the life of his grandson and set into motion an illustrious seven-decade long music career.

Pop was my hero because I knew he kept us from starving to death and he cared about me. He had three daughters, but I know he really wanted a son. I was his first grandson and like the son he never had, and he displayed his love and affection in various ways. When Dad walked out on us, Pop stepped in as my father figure, and was a man you could count on. I was fearful that something might happen to him, and realized if he did die, there was no way I was going to make it. Pop was my only means of survival as a child and I loved him with all my heart. As a boy, I always affectionately referred to him as, "Pop-Pop," but when I turned thirteen, he suggested I start calling him "Pop." I suppose he felt that using "Pop-Pop" was a little too boyish for my age.

I was twelve years old when Pop bought me my first guitar from a pawn shop. He played the mandolin beautifully and taught me how to play the guitar so that I could accompany him. For several enjoyable hours, we sat and played songs like, 'O Sole Mio,' or gospel songs. Pop's all-time favorite gospel song was, 'What a Friend We Have in Jesus.' I've treasured his mandolin and lovingly had it restored. I have no idea how old it is, but I do know that it was hand-carried across the ocean, and it was the one possession Pop loved most. I wish I could play it the way he did back then. He made you feel like you were right there sitting in Sicily. He had the movements when he played it that indicated he felt the music in his heart. In my eyes, Pop was my hero, my savior, and just a fantastic human being.

Practicing the guitar became Allen's passion and he did so every opportunity he had. One fateful day, a stranger walking by discovered this "Caged Bird" singing, and it was music to her ears.

When I was fourteen years old, I was practicing the guitar in my bedroom with the window open. I had an Eddy Arnold song book in front of me because I loved to play and sing his songs. This lady, who was temporarily living just a few doors up from us, was the wife of an Army Major. She stopped and stood outside and listened to me sing for a while. She approached the door and knocked, wanting to know if she was listening to a recording of sorts. Mom answered, 'No, that's my son practicing in his bedroom.' I was playing and I looked back and there was this lady whom I had never seen before. She was standing in the doorway listening to me sing. I stopped and she pleaded, 'No, no, no, please, go ahead and keep singing!' I finished the song and she remarked, 'You know, we're good friends with A. V. Tidmore, the owner of WPPA radio station. Maybe you can audition for him? I would love to have him hear you!'

She arranged for me to be taken to the remote fifty-thousand-watt station in Yorkville, Pennsylvania, referred to as "The Tower," where all recordings were made. I auditioned by playing a few songs, and the engineer was this cool guy who said, 'You know what? I am going to play this back for you.' He played the recording back to me and said, 'Now, you sound like Roy Rogers, don't you?' I had never heard myself recorded like that and was amazed. He asked me to make a list of all the songs I knew because A.V. Tidmore wanted to talk to me about coming on his radio show.

It wasn't long before I met with A.V. Tidmore who was a tall and sophisticated man. 'Listen, I'd like for you to have a half an hour radio show where you sing your songs and talk to people on the air. You think you could do that?' 'Yeah, I think I can.' I was scared to death because I wasn't sure if I could or not, but it seemed like something I should try. The station was important in its day, and it was Willie Whistle, the producer and radio personality that really put WPPA on the map. Anytime Willie traveled to Nashville, Tennessee, everyone recognized him as one of the best-known radio personalities around. A.V. Tidmore coached me, 'You're going to have to come up with a song that you start off every show with.' I chose 'I'm Sending You a Big Bouquet of Roses' because my idol, Eddy Arnold, had a big hit with that song, and I loved it so much. I'd say, 'This is Allen Karl coming to you live from WPPA Radio,' and then kicked off the show with that song.

Promo picture WPPA Radio, age 14

We encouraged and answered call-ins where fans could ask me questions. I answered and talked a bit and then told them I wanted to sing a song for them. It was a wonderful time, and I had a lot of fans in Pottsville and the surrounding towns. Female fans sent roses to the station with notes attached to them. I took the time to mention a couple of them during my show and thanked them for the beautiful roses. A lot of girls called me, and Mom got very disturbed about it and tried even harder to keep me sheltered. Surprisingly, a half an hour show went by quickly, but I enjoyed every minute of it. I am forever thankful to the Army Major and his wife. They not only discovered my talent, but also drove me to and from the radio station. Without their assistance, the radio show would not have been possible and who knows where I'd be today.

Allen at the WPPA Radio Station in Pottsville 2022

Altogether, Allen had his very own radio show for three years and then A.V. Tidmore encouraged him to move on to bigger and better things. He signed Allen up for a prominent talent show at the Santa Fe Ranch in nearby Reading, Pennsylvania. At seventeen, Allen won a local talent contest singing a Bobby Lord song called, 'I Can't Make My Dreams Understand.' His first-place win meant a one-year recording contract with King Records. The Santa Fe Ranch was a theme park owned by Shorty and Dolly Long and regular shows took place on the stage. Shows in theme parks were a big deal back then and drew large crowds and some of the biggest names in music. King Records was also owned and operated by Shorty Long who consequently shelved Allen's recording career but offered him the spotlight for the next four years as the opening act for some of the biggest names in country music. Stars like Patsy Cline, Eddy Arnold, Jean Shepard, Hawkshaw Hawkins, Wanda Jackson, Farron Young, Ferlin Husky, and more. Allen's first recorded song with King Records finally materialized in 1960 with a song called, 'You're the Reason.' The song did extremely well on the charts and all the radio stations picked it up. Allen's music career was off to a blazing start, and these theme park shows provided much needed family fun every weekend.

AUGUST, 1958

Shorty and Dolly Long
Owners of The Santa Fe Ranch
in Reading, PA

Competing for a recording contract
in a talent contest held at
The Santa Fe Ranch

Shows at The Santa Fe Ranch were held from May to early September which worked out perfectly with my school schedule. Nana was always pushing to get out on Sundays, and we made a day of it at the park. Pop drove us all and we grilled out hotdogs and hamburgers on a charcoal grill. When showtime rolled around, we left our things on the picnic table and found seats in the grandstand. Pop insisted on sitting as close to the stage as possible because he was truly my biggest fan

.

I remember singing with Jean Shepard and Hawkshaw Hawkins. Hawkshaw was this tall guy with a big hat and Jean was a beautiful young woman. They did such a wonderful job together. Wanda Jackson came backstage one night, and said, 'You know, I just wrote this song and I wanted to see what y'all think of it.' She reached for her guitar and began singing and everyone agreed she should record it. That's exactly what she ended up doing, and the song was called, 'Right or Wrong.' It became one of the biggest hits she ever had, and I loved to sing that song and still make it a part of my set list today. Never once did I consider myself to be something special up there on that stage, I was just incredibly lucky to be part of it all.

It was magical being with Patsy Cline up on stage. She was a woman way beyond her time, wearing a purple pantsuit back in 1958 when all women were supposed to look and act like June Cleaver. Patsy Cline was the flamboyant type, and she lit up the room when she entered and had a presence that was so rare to find. Whenever she walked into the room, everyone hushed, and I felt it with her more than any other big star. She also loved to chatter. What she was saying might not have been important, but her enthusiasm made you want to listen. This one show, Patsy had finished her set and went off stage. It was my turn, so I came out to the microphone and announced that I was going to sing, 'As Far as I'm Concerned.' To my surprise, Patsy walked right up beside me and announced, 'We're going to do this together.' I began the song, and she repeated the lyrics after me and harmonized all the while moving in closer and closer to me. Patsy scared the heck out of me that night. I was feeling extremely uncomfortable because I was only eighteen and not as worldly as she was. Patsy wrapped her arm around me! I was playing the guitar, trying not to forget the words, and my face was beet red. The audience laughed and clapped, and she knew exactly what to do to incite a riot – I mean the crowd went crazy and I was the only one feeling uncomfortable.

You know Patsy knew the audience loved our duet and she asked me if I'd consider opening for several more of her shows. It broke my heart when Mom told her I had other obligations and wouldn't be able to do that. To tour with Patsy Cline would have meant the world to me and I often wonder what my life would have been like If I had gone with her on tour.

Allen performing at The Santa Fe Ranch

As Allen found new life in his music, he began to see that there was an existence beyond the control and confinement of his mother's sickening ways. The proverbial train was now rolling along, picking up speed with each passing year, and it wouldn't be long before Allen could finally find the strength within himself to entirely break free from his mother's sovereignty.

13

That's Enough!

*"Positive people are not positive because they skated through life.
They're positive because they have been through hell
and decided they don't want to live there anymore."*
–Mona Lisa Nyman

Like the superstition that plagues most high-rise buildings, I considered skipping over chapter thirteen in this biography, but I just couldn't. To tell you the truth, thirteen is my favorite number. In fact, my great-grandfather was known as "The Man Who Made Thirteen Lucky," and he proudly displayed that title on his business card. Plus, I believe thirteen was an important transitional year in Allen's life because he was lucky to move away from the country and back to Pottsville where more opportunities existed. Allen's thirteenth year of life propelled him in an entirely new direction, where breaking away from a childhood of abuse now showed a glimmer of hope. Most importantly, Allen discovered the talent, wit, work ethic, and inner strength to deal with problems in his life coming from a single source – his mother. Essentially, Kitty was a black hole. No light radiated from her, and she pulled everyone around her into a twisted and chaotic world. At thirteen years old, Allen dug in at the event horizon and used the power of music and hard work to pry himself away from his mother's darkness-vowing to forever break the cycle of abuse in his own life and strive to be everything she was not.

*After my eleventh-grade year, Mom decided she was going to
leave the apartment Pop provided and move in with this lady*

named Annie living in Orwigsburg. It was a wrong decision, but she made bad decisions my entire life. Of course, my brother and I went with her, but we had no idea how she found this woman. Pop was against the idea, but Nana could care less because Mom was a real pain. Annie was this short woman with a large hunchback causing her to walk crooked. Mom and Annie were involved sexually, and we inadvertently walked in on them on more than one occasion. I saw things in my youth that are still branded in my mind to this day.

Jerry adds:

So many things we saw our mother do were just not normal like finding this lady living down in Orwigsburg. Our mother dragged us to that home, and we stayed there basically taking everything over, much to the chagrin of Annie's family. Mom ruled that lady like she ruled us and treated her badly. In fact, Mom should have been arrested and put behind bars for the way she treated all of us. She wasn't jailed, but the police did force us to leave the home, and Annie died shortly thereafter. I don't know how, but she died! It was a horrible thing. It was with total disregard that Mom packed up and moved us all into this lady's house. At that point, Allen had to catch the bus to Blue Mountain High School for his senior year, not knowing anybody! You see, Mom didn't care about the effects of anything on our lives. Our lives meant nothing to her except what she could physically force us to do for her. She was a serious embarrassment to us, but there was nothing we could do about it. We had to keep our noses out of it, and it wasn't bad enough to be treated the way we were, but to embarrass us on top of that! There was no recourse for us back then and we often wondered, 'Is there anyone else having to deal with what we're having to deal with?' We concluded that no, there wasn't.

The summer before Allen's senior year he took a job working at Zulick's Shoe Factory where it dawned on him that he could never lead the mundane life of a factory worker. He would never be content to do just one thing, every single day, the same way for his entire life. Contentment was never a word in Allen's vocabulary and the mundane would never be something for which he could settle. Allen yearned to create a multifaceted life as he now tried to cram several lifetimes into one. He understood that he could do many different things in life and be wildly successful.

I asked myself every day on that job, 'How can a man spend his life doing this?' The workers entered the building every day and placed their lunch pails in the same cubby hole. When it came time for lunch, everyone gathered at the same table, sat in the same seat, and when finished, returned to the exact same spot to work. The next morning workers entered the building at the same time and placed their lunch pails in the exact same cubby hole. It was the same mindless routine from day-to-day and I thought to myself, 'There is no way I would be content to do this for the rest of my life.'

Allen made the best of being uprooted for his senior year, finding new friends, and getting involved with a play that was modeled after the popular, 'Dick Clark's American Bandstand.' The play brought together the talent that would make up his very first band, The Shuffles.

I did a play my senior year modeled after 'Dick Clark's American Bandstand.' They wanted me to do a song from the top ten charts, called, 'A Lover's Plea,' by Mack Vickery. The guys in that show were all talented and we decided to come together and form our own band named The Shuffles. Our lead guitar player, Ken Rose decided on this name because he kicked off every show playing 'The Guitar Boogie Shuffle.' This was my very first band and we played rock-n-roll at high school dances and many other places. I really got into music, and it seemed like an entirely different world for me. The most I ever made with The Shuffles was ten dollars per night, so although I wanted to just do music, I still had to work my other job.

In the later part of 1959, Allen worked at Matey's Car Wash for a dollar and a quarter per hour which was the most money he made back then. Kitty owned a 1949 Plymouth and because she was too nervous to drive, she just left it sitting out front. Allen convinced her to let him trade it in on his first car. For seventeen hundred dollars he purchased a lightly used 1959 black and white Ford. Payments were thirty-eight dollars a month and he earned thirty-three dollars a week which his mother took most of. It didn't matter because the car was now Allen's way out of the house. The car offered him the freedom to go out, have friends, play gigs, go to work, and even date. He had never had the chance to meet girls before because Kitty was so overbearing. Allen was a handsome young man and girls were starting to take notice.

My first serious kiss came at the age of nineteen. Mom and Annie were out in the kitchen talking. The kitchen was located on the other side of the dining room and away from the living room where we were watching television. I was in my pajamas sitting next to one of Annie's relatives who was visiting while her husband and son were back home in New Jersey. I had never come on to a woman before in my life, but she was married with children and knew exactly what she wanted from me. Out of nowhere, she jumped on top of me and started kissing and coming on to me. Things got a little too hot and heavy, so I tossed her off me and onto the living room floor. She hit the floor with a thud, prompting Annie and Mom to call out, 'What's going on in there?' We both answered in unison, 'Nothing!' I sure didn't know what to think of all that, but I certainly didn't want to get her pregnant, so I had to do something to stop it.

Senior picture 1959

Allen was beginning to enjoy his newfound freedom and he was gaining strength and self-confidence with every job, musical performance, and interpersonal connection that he made apart from the pain inflicted by his "smother." Kitty had no respect for any man in her life, not even Pop. She consistently took advantage of his generous nature, always taking and never giving. She bullied and walked over every man in her life, because not one of them could set clear and concise boundaries with her. Not one person gathered the courage to stand up to Kitty and say, 'That's enough!' Allen finally changed all of that in one defining moment.

It was before my twentieth birthday when Mom and I got into an argument, and she tried to hit me like she had always done before. This time, I blocked the hit, and I grabbed her arms and slammed her up against the wall. I yelled, 'That's enough! That's enough! No more!' I know it scared her to death and I thought to myself, 'I am not going to hit you.' I could never hit her, but the terror on her face reassured me that I got my message across to her loud and clear. I finally got to her and thought, 'I'll bet I am not scaring you nearly as much as you have scared me throughout my entire life.' I simply turned and walked away. From that day on, she kept me away from my brother and tried convincing him that I was a devil he needed to stay away from. My brother and I didn't have much of a relationship until after I was married. After he left the Army and married Darlene's friend and co-worker Martha, we seemed to reunite. Our mom was the wedge between us for years and she tried everything in the world to keep us apart. My brother is a good person, and I was always willing to protect him, save his life, or do whatever I could for him.

Jerry Adds:

When Allen pushed Mom up against the wall, she retaliated by saying, 'Jerry, there's something terribly wrong with your brother. Promise me, you won't associate with him ever again!' I didn't promise her because there was no way I would promise that, so I just turned and walked away.

She was my mom, but she was a terrible mom, and I conquered my fear of her. It took standing up to her finally to set me free. After that moment, anything I did was on my own terms. I dictated what I was going to do in my life. Now I understood that I could stop it all at any time and she no longer exercised control over me. I took away her power when I slammed her up against the wall and walked out that door as a free man. She was no longer a threat to me so I could eventually accept her as my biological mother, of course, I used the term loosely. I cut the chains and she could never put them around me again. I wish I could say that I forgave my mom back then, but no, I don't think I've ever completely forgiven her because there was just too much to it.

After losing two years of his schooling because his mother kept him home, Allen graduated from Blue Mountain High School in 1960, just before he turned twenty-years-old. He continued to work various odd jobs and perform with The Shuffles, staying away from the house and his mother as much as possible. After a year or so, Annie and her family were fed up with Kitty's antics and physical abuse. The police were called to remove them from Annie's home and once again Pop came to their rescue. He brought them back to Pottsville to live in a home he bought for them at 1504 A Norwegian Street. Kitty started babysitting for extra cash and the apple certainly didn't fall too far from the tree. Like mother, like daughter, the methods of childcare were nothing short of appalling.

Senior yearbook photo

Mom took in children to babysit, and the moment the child's mother was out of sight, she would lock them in the closet, or tie them to the highchair in the kitchen. The poor child would be there all day and lived in that highchair, eating, sleeping, and playing. There may be a few toys on the tray, but nothing else. They could never run around the place, and she never held or comforted the child because she just had no love, concern, or patience for any of it. She always knew when the child's mother was due to return and quickly untied the child and deceptively smiled and handed the child over to the mother. Mom could be so convincing at times, and no one would ever suspect her of any wrongdoing.

After graduation Allen found a job at a local feed company and continued performing at local dances and venues. One of the most popular local venues they regularly played was Willow Lake. The owner's daughter went to a different high school than Allen, but they started seeing each other. The relationship was a rollercoaster of emotions because it was off and on, and it was well known that she was seeing someone else on the side. The tumultuous relationship directly affected The Shuffle's bookings at Willow Lake. If the relationship was on then so was the band, if not, then another band took their place.

Back then I was dating a girl and her parents owned Willow Lake. At the time, I needed someone to be serious about me although I was green and had no knowledge of women. It really bothered me that the relationship was so on and off again. It was emotional and it hurt to learn that she was seeing someone else on the side. We played Willow Lake for four weeks in a row and then suddenly the Jordan Brothers took it over and we were out. I never really understood why we had to leave, but it was all relative to whether we were together as a couple. The guys in the band pressured me to keep things going just so we could book the gig.

Allen was now working steadily at the feed company and overall, his life was headed in the right direction until a thoughtless mistake altered the course of his life forever.

I worked for a local feed company on a farm, and I needed to make a car payment of thirty-eight dollars. I remember my boss had all sorts of rifles there at the company, standing up against the wall. I honestly didn't think he would miss one for a week, so I borrowed a rifle and took it to the pawn shop. I hocked it with the intention that when I got paid the following week, I would get it out of hoc and replace it on the rack. My boss did notice that the rifle was missing and reported it to the police. They found the rifle at the pawn shop and connected it to me. I was never arrested or went to court, but I was fired, and the police presented me with an ultimatum. I could avoid jail and maintain a clean record if I joined the military. I had no choice in the matter because I didn't want this on my permanent record, so I accepted their terms. I was afraid to leave my little brother with my mom at that time, but now, there was nothing I could do about it. You know that one mistake has stayed with me my entire life. There was just no excuse whatsoever for doing what I did, and I have never forgiven myself for it.

Allen dreamed of becoming an aviator one day. As a boy, he built plastic model airplanes and suspended them by wire and thumbtack in various flying positions from his bedroom ceiling. There was no required entrance exam for the Army or Marines, but the Navy and Air Force had one. Allen took the Air Force entrance exam and kept his fingers crossed that he would pass. Either way, he knew that he would be leaving Pottsville for basic training and began tying up the loose ends.

14

Be a Good Soldier

"Life is tough, but darling ... so are you!"
–Stephanie Bennett Henry

Allen's life and future were hanging in the balance, and which direction life would take him was at the mercy of the Air Force entrance exam. Allen didn't know where he was headed, but he certainly knew he was on his way. He was scared that he might fail the exam, so when he received news that he passed with excellence, he felt an enormous relief.

A couple of weeks before being sworn into service, Allen thought enough of his on again, off again girlfriend, to propose. He wanted to know that he had a girl waiting for him back home. It was more of a promise than a wedding ring, like putting a deposit on something. They didn't have a set date and in hindsight Allen knew that it was a young and foolish thing to do.

A sizable Halloween dance in the street was the last show Allen would ever play with The Shuffles. The band broke apart and the members headed in different directions. At the age of twenty-one, Allen was officially enlisted in the United States Air Force on November 23rd, 1961. Standing outside the bus bound for basic training, the moment was bittersweet.

Of course, Nana wasn't there. Mom was crying while Pop hugged me tight. He always had the habit of grabbing me by my cheek, and with tears filling his eyes he said, 'Look, you just be a good soldier.' I chose a window seat and as I was waving goodbye, I focused on my brother. He was just crying his eyes out and that vision of him still haunts me to this day. It made me feel so bad and I wanted to get off the bus, hug him and take care of him again, but I didn't have a choice. I had to go, but I spent hours on that bus anguishing over the whole thing and will never forget his face as the bus pulled away from the station. My poor brother was stuck there, and I couldn't save him, but at least he was high school age and not that frail little kid anymore.

The Shuffles' last performance photo 1960

The Shuffles at their 62nd High School Reunion
Left to right: Allen, Bill Orf, and Ken Rose.
Drummer Jerry Reber not pictured here

Jerry recounts the time he had to spend in the absence of his big brother:

I know without Allen I wouldn't be here today. I would not have survived by myself. Allen, being the older and stronger one, saved me so many times from near death. Even though he was gone for four years of my life, he was there when a big brother was truly needed. Allen's four-year absence was pure hell for me, and you know, Nana was no help whatsoever. Between Nana and Mom, my life was fully controlled without the support of Al. He was fortunate enough to be born almost five years before me. I was glad he was able to make it out, but during the time he was gone, it was all on me.

There were times during the school year that I couldn't attend my classes. Mom called me home because she and Nana had a terrible fight, or she didn't feel that Nana could help her like I could. If she felt she was going to die or there was something terrible that was going to happen to her, or she couldn't reach that whack doctor of hers in California. He was a naturalist and did absolutely nothing but run up a telephone bill she couldn't pay. We were constantly in debt. We went to Woolworth's, and she'd steal just enough stuff to put in a bag and be caught as we were exiting the store. She'd talk the cop out of it by telling a lie, 'It must have fallen in the bag or Jerry, did you put that in my bag?' She was a constant embarrassment for me. A constant embarrassment! She couldn't give us credit for anything and when Allen went away, I thought, 'My God, I don't know how in the world I'm going to survive with him being gone.'

At sixteen, I remember Allen boarding the bus for basic training in Texas. We looked at each other and I knew what he was thinking, but Mom was standing right there, and he couldn't say anything. I know he was thinking, 'Jerry, do whatever it takes to survive. I love you and you will be in my thoughts and prayers.' I know he really was feeling incredibly sorry. It was just the two of us, then suddenly, there was just one of us. He was free and I was still trapped. I was trapped! I got a bloody nose several times and I still get bloody noses. To this day, my nose is so crooked with a huge lump because it's been broken a couple of times. Mom hit me good one time and got my nose bleeding. It hurt so bad, I swear it was broken, but she wouldn't let me go to the doctor. There's not much you can do with a broken nose anyway, but then she did the worst thing imaginable.

I was eighteen at the time my mother encouraged the lady living downstairs to come to my bedroom one night. My bedroom was located on the third floor, and she sent this lady upstairs to crawl into bed with me! I had enough presence of mind to throw her out of bed and yell, 'Get out of here!' 'Yeah, but your mom said that you would be willing to...' It just substantiates the sickness that this woman had, and I am sorry I ever called her my mother. As soon as I graduated high school, I left and got as far away from her as possible.

Allen arrived at basic training in San Antonio, Texas and quickly discovered that he had been in training for this moment all his life. Kitty was the epitome of the drill sergeant throughout his childhood, which made military basic training a stroll in the park for him. The training was designed to be challenging both mentally and physically, but ultimately it transformed modest recruits into confident airmen with the skills necessary to survive.

I was really surprised when I was sworn in and they were shaking my hand and people were so nice and kept telling me, 'You're going to enjoy your stay with the Air Force.' I thought, 'Wow, I've really made the right decision here.' I arrived at the base and the minute we got off the bus, they had us line up. There were guys from New York with long hair and the next thing I know, this technical instructor was walking down the line screaming in everyone's face. Telling us how we are nothing and lower than whale scum in the ocean, and I thought, 'What happened?' The instructor shouted in my face too, and I just stood at attention and thought, well, this is nothing new. I can manage this, even though it was surprising. I don't care what you dish out, I can handle it.

Of course, I spent years learning how to make my bed. Mom always insisted that I did it wrong and she'd tear the bedding apart and make me redo it repeatedly. When you enter the military as a basic recruit, they want to mold you into what they see as a good soldier – a good airman. To do that, you must be able to take orders and not only that, but you must be capable of completing those orders exactly as instructed. That is what I had been doing all my life, so the military for me was a dream. 'Oh my gosh, pour it on! I can take so much more than you got!' I showed them that I could take it and they were shocked. In fact, I was the best that they had ever seen in basic training. If they said, 'Jump this high.' I jumped that high or higher, no matter what, and it was so automatic and natural for me. I didn't question anything and did it exactly the way they wanted. They insisted that my socks had to be folded up a certain way and placed two inches from my shorts. Everything had to be perfect. They examined my footlocker and remarked, 'My God, after being told only one time!' 'Yes, Sir. YES, SIR!' 'How could this man come away from his family and be so disciplined?' Well, it was nothing new for me. They called me aside wanting me to be the Dorm Chief because I was able to understand everything they were trying to teach immediately after they taught it. I was quickly promoted as Dorm Chief in charge of *everybody, ensuring each soldier completed his tasks just the way they should. I excelled at this and overall enjoyed my stay in basic training.*

Shortly after arriving on base, we all had our heads shaved so everyone looked the same, but we didn't all learn at the same speed. Early in the morning, I heard the unmistakable sound of the technical instructors coming up the wooden steps. When they turned the lights on, you'd better be up, ready, and standing at attention next to your bunk. I'd be standing at the head of my bunk ready for inspection in my shorts, and there were guys still sleeping. The instructors flipped over their beds sending the guys flying! Bam! They'd hit the floor hard, but I mean, you learned; your butt had better be out of that bed when the lights came on. I coached my guys, 'Listen to me! When they come up those steps, be ready because this is for real!'

I was successful in getting my dorm back in shape and all throughout basic training because I grew up with an abusive and controlling mom. Reading her was a matter of survival. After a while you know that's a copperhead snake, don't touch it. You learn because you must learn to survive. How much are you going to get hurt and feel pain before you learn? Early on my mom taught me some tough lessons. I watched her face and when she glanced at something, I looked at that same something. I discovered that I shouldn't just ignore this in life. If they are looking at something it is because they are not happy with it, so quickly do something about it, before they break out on you. I had to do that every single day, so my dysfunctional childhood made my Air Force basic training a breeze.

After eight weeks, Allen transferred to Chanute Air Force Base located outside Rantoul and Champaign, Illinois for flight training. It was there he learned crucial systems such as the autopilot, evasive maneuver, and the system that prevented his plane from being shot down. Flares were launched to throw off the enemy's missiles which reacted to the flare's heat instead of the heat coming from their plane. Six months later, Allen returned home to visit with friends and family before heading out as far away from home as he could travel.

McGuire Air Force Base was entirely too close to my mom, so I wanted to go to Japan to finish my flight training, and that's exactly what I did. The Air Force has what is called, Temporary Duty Assignments (TDY). Throughout my military career with four years on active duty and two years on reserves, I was stationed at the following Air Force bases: Hickam, Hawaii, Osan, Korea, Clark, Philippines, Udorn, Thailand, De Nang and Tan Son Nhut in Vietnam, Kadina, Okinawa, and Ramey, Puerto Rico. These were all TDY, but my main base station was in Yokota, Japan. With these assignments you traveled back and forth spending three months here, and maybe four months there. I was temporarily stationed in Okinawa and spent a good deal of my time in the far east, but my primary bases included Lackland, Texas, Chanute, Illinois, Yokota, Japan, and Shaw in South Carolina.

United States Air Force

While Allen completed training, things weren't working out with his girl back home. The relationship with his first serious girlfriend ended and his ring was returned.

My girlfriend back home wasn't the person I could count on to be serious about me, and I honestly don't think she ever really loved me. I could see that and was glad it worked out the way it did. I am sure my mom was instrumental in our separation because she constantly took advantage of her asking to be driven to places and do things for her. My girlfriend saw a trend she didn't necessarily want to deal with if she was married to me. After six months of an engagement, she dropped her ring off at my Aunt Jeanette's house and ran off with someone else.

Allen's existence up to this point had been wickedly cruel, but Japan was far away from Pottsville and offered him the freedom to learn, explore, love, and play music.

15

The Sweetheart Tree

"They say there's a tree in the forest, a tree that will give you a sign. Come along with me to the Sweetheart Tree, come and carve your name next to mine. They say if you kiss the right sweetheart, the one you've been waiting for, big blossoms of white will burst into sight, and your love will be true ever more."
–Mancini/Mercer

A llen thrived while on active duty in Japan and melded easily with the multifaceted culture. He also found himself a valuable member of two squadrons that helped to define his military career.

At first, I was transferred to Yokota Air Force Base where they housed the F-102 planes, and I was assigned to that squadron called the F-102 Delta Darts. There were Russian Migs that would fly over our runway and buzz us because Russia was close to where we were in Japan. Our F-102 Delta Darts gave those Migs a lesson when we escorted them back to Russia. They positively understood they were up against modern technology that they didn't want to mess with. After that, the Russians never buzzed us again. When I was at Osan Air Force Base, we switched over from the F-102 to the Voodoo which was either an RF-101 reconnaissance plane or an F-101 jet fighter. I had the opportunity to fly second seat in both and our squadron was known as the Voodoo Men.

Allen overlooking Nagasaki, Japan

Allen finished his flight training at Yokota and in his free time he continued to search for ways to grow personally. Everything interested him, and he gobbled up all that life in a foreign country had to offer. He enrolled in aeronautical and electronics courses through extensions offered by the University of Maryland and became semi-fluent in Japanese.

I donated my time teaching English at Sophia University in Tokyo and thoroughly enjoyed that. I gathered seven students at a time in different tea houses, to discuss topics in Japanese and English. The conversation and total immersion into the culture and language was how I became semi-fluent in Japanese.

Adoring outdoor adventures, he climbed to the seventh station on the highest mountain in Japan called Mount Fuji. There are only ten stations total from the ground to the summit and the seventh station is two stations higher than the mountain's paved road could reach.[20] Wanting to evolve in mind and body, Allen spent an incredible amount of time dedicated to achieving his first-degree black belt in Karate. A black belt is exceedingly difficult to obtain because it is the highest level a Karateka can achieve.[21] Allen's black belt training started in Korea, continued in Japan, and was accomplished in the Philippines.

In addition to all of this, music stayed at the forefront of his life, and he put together a band called, The Dixieland Playboys. Musically speaking, the situation couldn't have been any better for Allen. He performed next to some of the biggest names in country music at the second largest Grand Ole Opry in the world located in Tokyo. His band was in high demand throughout Japan and subsequently made Allen the heartthrob of many women.

A lead singer of a popular band doesn't have to look extremely far to find many opportunities for one-night stands. Allen was propositioned every time he took the stage, and mostly by married women whose husbands were away on assignment. Allen's morality steered him clear of those traps. Instead, he was loyal to the Master Sargent's daughter. She was a beautiful blond-haired person stationed in Japan with her family. Every guy at the base was so jealous that Allen was dating her and bringing her along to every gig he played. Although the relationship stayed strictly platonic, they dated for several years; eventually showing off an engagement ring. However, a firm marriage date was never set because Allen was usually away on assignment and his fiancé was an emotional mess. She often seemed manic depressive, talking about dying, but other times she could be the life of the party. Although Allen dated one girl throughout his time in Japan, he came to realize that he wasn't truly "in love," and when it came time to transfer to Shaw Airforce Base in South Carolina, Allen called off the engagement altogether. However, wonderful new friends, experiences, and a fiancé were not the only things he would leave behind.

I bought a 1956 blue and white two-toned Ford in Japan that I parked on the base. It was beautiful and I loved that car so much. It had what was called a "Y" tag on it. Any car with that tag was not allowed to leave Japan, so when the time came to say goodbye forever, I gifted my Ford to a friend and fellow soldier. Of course, he was thrilled, but I am sure he wished he could have had my girl to go with it.

"Engaged" Master Sergeant's daughter

While stationed in Japan Allen was the lead singer for The Dixieland Playboys. Composed of five, extraordinarily talented, American soldiers, they played some of the best country music on the island nation. Growing in popularity, the band graced the stage at various bases and officer's clubs throughout the area as well as the prestigious venue known as the second largest Grand Ole Opry in the world. The Dixieland Playboys performed with the best, including modern-day Jimmy Rogers, Ferlin Husky, Hank Snow, and Johnny Cash.

Allen spent time with Johnny Cash in Japan and the two of them became good friends. Years later back in the states, Hank Snow sponsored Allen on the Gospel Hour at the Grand Ole Opry in Nashville,

Tennessee. The connections made early on in music were priceless and fueled his powerful desire to make performing a life-long career.

The Dixieland Playboys (Allen far right)

I played music with Johnny Cash in Tokyo and several other places, and we got to know each other well. I remember John loved Japanese food and we would get something to eat at an outside café and just talk for hours. Johnny was so open with nothing hidden about him. He could enjoy anything, and I remember we were spending time together at this place and John was throwing darts. He said, 'How much money are you gonna put on this dart?' I replied, 'Johnny, I'm not betting.' Luckily, I didn't bet because he was a particularly good dart thrower. He skillfully placed his darts anywhere he wanted to on a dartboard. It was just the trivial things like that, but we always had an enjoyable time when we were together. Unfortunately, we never reconnected in the states like we thought we would, but we had a wonderful time while overseas.

Allen's musical endeavors continued in Thailand where he was on TDY at Udorn Air Force Base. Allen fronted an all-Thai rock and roll band regularly playing the Thai owned, Miami Club. The bond that he and his Thai bandmates shared during that time was remarkable and proved to be some of the best years of his life. Forced to leave Thailand to join the fight in Vietnam, Allen's Thai friends gave him a grand send-off. In a sacred ceremony, they baptized him into Buddhism and gave him a going away gift to treasure.

Promo for Miami Club   Allen's all Thai Rock-N-Roll band

The four guys in the band and I grew close. I still have a photo that the lead guitar player gave to me. He wrote on the back, 'For the best friend to me, Al Sterner,' signed in 1965 by Anthorn Kanithasunthorn. The guys were always trying to get me to eat a popular snack food called Rice Bugs. These "snacks" are ten times larger than a cockroach and kept alive and for sale in glass containers. For just five Thai Bahts, which is the equivalent of fifteen cents today, you could reach into the glass jar and catch one. You hold the bug in your hand with its legs all sticking out through your fingers wiggling around. Then you bite the head off, squeeze their insides into your mouth, and throw away the shell. No matter how hard they tried to get me to do this, I just couldn't stomach it, so I was never fully, "Thai qualified."

When I was headed back to Vietnam, my bandmates held a beautiful ceremony for me. It was very touching, and it took two hours with singing, rituals, and glowing candlelight. It was very emotional, and they baptized me as a Buddhist and gave me a soft, twenty-four-carat gold necklace, with a buddha on it. I still have the necklace, but once we said our goodbyes after the ceremony, I never saw any of my Thai friends again.

After four years on active duty and two years in active reserves, Allen was granted leave on just three occasions. Once from Carswell Air Force Base in Fort Worth, again from Chanute Airforce Base near Rantoul, Illinois, and the last leave was from Shaw Air Force Base near Sumpter, South Carolina. One thing Allen wanted to do while back home in Pottsville, was reconnect with his estranged father who abandoned him so many years ago.

I never saw my dad again until I was twenty-one. From that little boy he left behind at four and a half years old, he never tried to get back in touch with me. After I finished with flight training, I asked my aunts and uncles to help me find him again. I was going off to Vietnam and I wanted to see him just in case I didn't get back. They found him and talk about the skeletons in closets. They knew all along where he was and just never told me. He was living in New Jersey, and they took me there to see him. It was very strange to think that I was going to visit this man who was my hero and left me as a little boy. I don't know exactly why he left me, but now I was going to see him again after all those years.

Dad was expecting me and walked out of the house and towards the car where I was. I got out, walked up to him, and instead of hugging each other, we shook hands and I said, 'I'm Allen.' He smiled, 'Yes, I know. Welcome.' His wife Florence came out of the house but stayed in the background. She was his

second wife and they never had children. My Aunt Doris got
out of the car and asked Karl if he would like to go with us and
get something to eat.

Allen and Karl in Titusville, NJ Circa 1963

We all went to this little diner, but we never had much to say.
I wanted to ask him so many questions, but then my family was
there, and it just felt like it wasn't as private as I needed it to be. I
didn't ask him any questions, like why did you leave me? That
never came up and we ended up returning to the house. We got
out of the car and shook hands again. He said, 'I'll pray for you
going to Vietnam.' I thanked him for that and watched him walk
back to his house. As we pulled away, I turned my head around
and looked out the window thinking he would turn and wave, but
he didn't. He just walked away just as he had done years ago.

Allen certainly wasn't raised with a keen sense of what love meant,
and the right girl hadn't come along with whom he felt a powerful
connection to, or had she? His soulmate was there all along, and
although they lost contact for several years when life pulled them in
different directions, what is meant to be will always find a way. Allen
was about to be hit with a breath of fresh air.

When my tour was over in Japan, I was able to travel back to Pennsylvania and that's when I reconnected with Darlene. We lost contact in high school because we attended separate schools. She attended a Seventh Day Adventist school called Blue Mountain Academy in Hamburg, Pennsylvania and I went to Blue Mountain High School in Cressona. My mom invited Darlene and her mother Laura over for a chicken pot pie dinner. Just back from Japan and still in uniform I came through the front door, and it was really comforting to find Darlene hiding behind it. I hadn't seen her for several years and my little playmate was now a grown woman. She jumped out to surprise me and I hugged her. We spent a lot of time together during that leave.

We went to Dorney Park in Allentown together and shared an ice cream cone. I never thought twice about licking the same cone because as children we used to swap chewed bubblegum and there was just a comfort that we had with one another even back then. That day, I begged her to go on a rickety, wooden rollercoaster ride with me and she initially refused. I said, 'Aw, c'mon! Let's get on this. What do you have to be scared about? I am the one going off to Vietnam.' With that, she finally agreed to ride it with me, and she was terrified. I was talking the whole way, telling her to put her arms up in the air and let go of the handle. She was white knuckled and way too scared to even scream. When it was over, I said, 'Let's go! Let's do it again!' There was no way she was going to ride it again, but we had the time of our lives together those few weeks.

The day before I had to leave to go back to Shaw Air Force Base and then back to Vietnam for a second tour of duty, we had a huge family picnic. Darlene and I sat under this big, beautiful tree, and just talked for the longest time. We carved our initials into that tree and dubbed it the "Sweetheart Tree" after a popular song on the radio. I knew at that moment, if I lived through it, we would get married. I fell in love with her, and she was such a breath of fresh air in my life. I often wonder if that tree is still there, but that was many years ago. The tree may be gone, but the memory of that day with Darlene, will live in my mind forever.

Darlene faithfully wrote to me in Vietnam and sent goodie boxes with cookies and all kinds of other things that she made. This same girl who introduced me to Jesus and Christianity also sent me "The Voice of Prophecy," which is a Seventh-Day Adventist course designed by HMS Richards.[22] I completed the course while I was over in Vietnam, and I sent it back to her. The course and Darlene both helped to bring me closer to God and be a much better person overall.

Dorney Park ice cream with Darlene

Headed back to Vietnam for a second TDY, Allen was about to witness first-hand the unimaginable atrocities of war. Darlene's understanding, patience, and absolute love for Allen, helped pull him through. For the first time in his life, he had a wonderful woman and a future full of promise.

16

Blood on the Ground

*"Fighting for Old Glory with gunfire all around, they fell
by the thousands, leaving their blood on the ground."*
–Allen Karl

The Delta Darts Squadron in Yakota, Japan.
Allen is standing in the middle-back row.

llen returned to Vietnam for his second and last TDY and
altogether spent thirteen, non-consecutive, months serving
there. His second assignment threw him into the middle of a situation
that was deteriorating, and the fight was heating up not only in
Vietnam but also back home in the United States. Anti-war protests,
and the overall discontent of the American people with the entire

situation, prompted the government to change its tactics. The government used soldiers like Allen, stationed primarily outside of Vietnam, to keep the true number of American soldiers being sent into the area concealed from public eye.

The first time I was ordered to Vietnam, my primary station was Yokota, Japan, but for the second tour, my primary station was Shaw Air Force Base in South Carolina. The reason the government would send TDY through Vietnam was because at the time, they were trying to reduce the appearance of large numbers of soldiers being sent to fight the war. TDYs were just a joke that the government was pulling on the American people and by that time, people were rioting in the streets and protesting our involvement altogether. If we had primary duty stations other than Vietnam, the president could send us in, and it didn't appear that he was escalating the war by sending additional forces. They got away with sending thousands of troops using this strategy.

As an airman on flying status, Allen flew second seat operating electronic counter measures on reconnaissance missions as part of a squadron called the Voodoo Men. This squadron was responsible for exploring and taking pictures of areas to obtain information about enemy forces, the terrain, and other military activities. They flew low and were escorted by at least one F-105 Thunderchief because they had no way of defending themselves if they came under enemy fire. Fighting intensified, the casualties were mounting up, and every day the reality of lost comrades was increasingly evident.

Many of our reconnaissance planes were shot down in the line of duty. We attended a briefing at five in the morning and then ate breakfast before taking off on our missions. During breakfast, we disciplined ourselves to not look at the people around us because there was a good chance when we returned that night, those same seats would be empty. I personally never wanted to know who was sitting next to me. I never wanted to look in their eyes, and I certainly never asked about their families. You didn't want to know if they were married or how many kids they had, because the less you knew about them, the better.

My role mostly involved taking pictures and our RF-101 Voodoo was equipped with five Eastman Kodak cameras. These cameras were connected to an air speed compensator and altimeter, so that once we reached a certain altitude and airspeed, the cameras automatically started clicking off and photographing in all directions. The F-105 Thunderchief escorted us as we took our photos and dropped the canisters back at the base for intelligence to go over. If we had to return to the same area, that was a tough time because the enemy threw everything but the kitchen sink at us. They didn't want us to re-take pictures over what we overlooked the first time.

Our plane was shot several times, but luckily the hydraulic systems and components weren't hit. One time we had a blown tire with smoke billowing out and had to make it all the way back to Da Nang Air Force Base, which was a real hotspot of intense fighting. I also took part in the 333 Combat Tactical Air Command in Da Nang, which meant you had to be ready to go anywhere, at any time, no matter where the hot spot was or where the problems popped up.

The Bronze Star is awarded to members of the United States Armed Forces for either heroic achievement or meritorious service in a combat zone.[23] Allen earned his Bronze Star in the field from his superior officers for his quick reaction to an emergency on base, saving the lives of three soldiers.

The Bronze Star was awarded to me after the base was hit by mortars, severely damaging a Quonset hut with three men still trapped inside. It was a terrible night. Everything was on fire and the hut was completely caved-in around these men. I grabbed one of the emergency axes near us and struck the hut from the outside. I did this repeatedly until I made a large enough opening to rescue those three men. I pulled two men to safety and another soldier saved the third. We were all so relieved to make it out of there alive and there's no doubt in my mind that these men would have perished without our quick reaction.

Allen's life-long dream to fly planes came true when there was a shortage of pilots and the commander moved Allen from second seat to first seat in a supersonic jet fighter. He took the main controls and it felt completely natural for him to be flying at extremely high speeds.

I went up initially in the RF-101 Voodoo and trained for autopilot systems and electronic counter systems, so if the pilot died, I could land the plane safely. After numerous missions, and with a shortage of pilots, my superiors wanted me to fly first seat. His actions followed the chain of command and were based upon a recommendation from my first seat pilot who vouched for me as being more than capable. I wouldn't have had the advantage of flying had I not been in Vietnam, because I was not sanctioned as a pilot to fly. The shortage created an opportunity, and I had a knack for it and took to it very well. I did receive additional training, but it's important to note that I was never sanctioned to be a pilot. Extreme circumstances allowed for extreme measures. The whole experience of flying a supersonic jet is like none other, and I felt like I was born to do it. Any rollercoaster ride could never come anywhere close to it.

Allen was now considered true Air Force flying status, but tragically, this dream became his worst nightmare. What he witnessed during an early morning mission one day, branded images in his mind that could never be erased.

It was only my second time carrying the liquid fire called Napalm. The first time I carried it, we used it over the dense jungles of Vietnam to create space between our American Marine forces and the Viet Cong closing in on their position. Approximately one hundred and seventy-seven Marines were pinned up against the Mekong Delta. We told the Marine's radio man that we were coming in hot at treetop level. We wanted our forces down there to huddle up as close as possible because we were going to drop Napalm and light up the jungle. When you come in at tree top level at a high speed, no one can hear you coming. If you happen to look in the right direction, you might be able to see two jets, but you can't hear them until they pass over. The air then comes together and clashes with a boom like thunder after lightning. Prior to that, I was only flying reconnaissance missions with no way to protect myself or my wingman. I flew nine missions altogether as the first seat pilot, but there were many others that I completed in second seat.

I will never forget we received intelligence about a building at specific coordinates believed to be where the Viet Cong were storing munitions and armaments. Our orders were to neutralize that building with Napalm. It was early in the morning when we reached our target area and I wanted to do a fly over. The building was in the open and something about that didn't feel right to me. I told my wingman that something didn't look right, and that I wanted to take a second look with another pass over. With all missions, Da Nang Air Force Base was listening in and monitoring our entire conversation. Da Nang got in my headphones barking orders for us to immediately hit the target rather than fly over again. Although fuel was running low, I insisted on one more pass over and my wingman was getting upset with me too. I am sure he thought I was losing my nerve, and I just knew Da Nang was thinking they should never have let me take the first seat. They must have been thinking that I wasn't ready because I was "choking" up there.

It was crazy and confusing all at the same time because if I didn't obey orders, I could face a court-martial. People were shouting orders into our headphones so on our third pass, we dropped the Napalm. Immediately I asked my wingman if there was a secondary, which meant an explosion. If the building was truly housing munitions, there should have been an enormous explosion. He replied, 'Negative.' When we circled back around and eyed the target, there were dozens of children on fire and running in every direction! Unable to get the Napalm off their bodies, they were dropping to the ground like flies. Horrified, I cried out into my headphones, 'Oh my God! What have I done!' Intelligence made an awful mistake. The building we neutralized was not housing Viet Cong munitions. It was a school filled with young children, and the open space I questioned was their playground.

The part I couldn't make sense of with all the chatter in my ear was that the Viet Cong would have had munitions covered and camouflaged and not at a building out in the open. Our target wasn't hidden, and nothing added up and that is why I was insisting on more flyovers before dropping the Napalm. I returned to base visually upset and my commanding officer said, 'Look, you have to understand these children were simply casualties of war.' In other words, no one was to blame. I've suffered countless flashbacks and nightmares reliving that day. In my mind, I can still see the images of those burning children and it haunts me. Even now, whenever I fly commercially, I can't sit in a window seat. No, I'll never do that again for the rest of my life. My deepest desire to fly was given to me, but I've spent the rest of my life living in remorse.

Allen flying first seat reconnaissance over Vietnam

A Purple Heart Medal is a United States military decoration awarded in the name of the President to those wounded or killed while serving.[24] This prestigious military award was bestowed upon Allen because of the injuries he sustained in hand-to-hand combat with a young Vietnamese soldier.

We received intelligence that there would be a sabotage attack on our planes, and being undermanned at the time, we needed to sit by our planes to guard them. Resting near the landing gear of our plane, a young Vietnamese soldier surprised me. I suppose we startled one another, because when I turned around, he saw me and the only thing he could do was react by swinging the butt of his gun at me. His gun struck me in the face, busted in my facial features, and sent me back against the landing gear. He pulled his rifle around to shoot me, but I drew my .45 pistol first. I fired three fatal shots in defense, but I have been very troubled over that for years. The blow he delivered opened me up and required twenty-five stitches inside my mouth. I lost all my teeth in the upper and lower parts on the left side and so they performed plastic surgery at Clark Air Force Base in the Philippines.

Proudly serving America in The United States Air Force since 1961, Allen was up for reenlistment while actively serving in Vietnam. It was 1965 and his life up to this point was all about obeying orders both from his mother and his superior officers. All prior decisions were motivated by what made others happy and were based solely on what everyone else wanted. It was now up to Allen to decide what was best for *his* future and long-term aspirations. The realization that neither the Vietnamese nor the Americans were content with his service efforts, compelled him to leave the service and return to civilian life in the United States.

In Vietnam, Hanoi Hannah was on the radio constantly telling us how our wives and girlfriends were back home with other people, and we were wasting our time being there. Basically, we were wasting our time there. Vietnam is something I will never be proud of, because after all those years and countless soldiers slaughtered on both sides, it was all for nothing. I was gung-ho at first, like everyone else, until I realized that you're not wanted in an area that you are supposed to protect. Suddenly, you are ordered there and realize no one wants you in Vietnam, and they don't even want you back in the United States. So, where do we go? What are we supposed to do? It's a terrible feeling when your own compatriots don't want you, and now we were stuck between two worlds all because of one place that I was in. I remember landing at Travis Air Force Base in California when Americans were rioting in the streets and protesting the Vietnam War. People called us names, accused us of killing women and children, threw trash at us, cursed us, and labeled us warmongers.

I served my country in multiple locations, not just in Vietnam. I love my country and I am proud to have served in the Air Force, but I am saddened it all turned out the way that it did.

When we came back home, no one was there thanking us for our service and welcoming us back. It's a sad time in our country's history. You know, I have never asked my government for one thing that I was entitled to as a Veteran. I paid for my own college, I never applied for a VA loan, medical care, or anything else. If I hadn't been in Vietnam when my time came up to re-enlist, more than likely I would have. After my childhood and four years of service, I certainly had no problems following orders. Anywhere else in the world would have been a piece of cake and I knew that I would have been promoted. They promised promotion along with more money, but it just wasn't worth it to be in Vietnam anymore. I came back to my home base at Shaw in South Carolina, and I was officially released from active duty in the military on November 23, 1965, with an Honorable Discharge.

After Vietnam, Allen struggled with life as a civilian. He tried to maintain his sanity by pulling on coping mechanisms he developed as a child. Allen came home with a mosquito-borne infectious disease that tormented him with long bouts of severe chills followed by intense sweating. Although he was treated with Quinine, it took years to be completely clear of the symptoms. In addition to the physical struggles of Malaria, the traumatic events created a mental health crisis as Allen faced PTSD (Post Traumatic Stress Disorder). He suffered months of terrible dreams and flashbacks and retreated to that special place in his mind, but he knew he had to get through it somehow.

When I landed safely at Shaw Air Force Base, finally home from Vietnam, everyone had a wife, girlfriend, or family member there to greet them, except me. Everyone was so happy and hugging, but I had no one to welcome me home. That stung a little, because I thought at the very least Darlene could have been there waiting for me. I thought she would drive to South Carolina to meet me since I was finally getting out of the service and that was where I landed. I was mad and hurt, thinking she may have had second thoughts about us based on a letter I received from Pop. I know she had been spending a great deal of time with my brother Jerry, and I wondered if they had strong feelings for one another. I certainly didn't want to cause any confrontation with him or Darlene. So, I decided to stay in South Carolina and pursue my music instead. I was the lead singer for a band called the Southern Hilltoppers and we played five or six nights all throughout South Carolina. I lived with my lead guitar player and his family, rent free. I was fishing, singing, and really enjoying myself. He had a lovely daughter who spent time with me shopping for clothes because the only clothes I had were my military outfits. At the time, she was engaged to a guy in college, and we never hugged, held hands, or anything, so I thought we were just friends. We did have fun together and I enjoyed my time with her, but my attention was quickly brought back to Darlene.

In December, Pop wrote to me concerned because Darlene was dating and he hinted strongly that if we meant anything to one another, it would be in my best interest to return home as soon as possible. Pop watched the two of us grow up and he always thought the world of Darlene, fondly referring to her as his "Baby Doll." Pop meant so much to me and I knew all along that he really wanted me to marry her, so I returned for Christmas, and she and I reconnected. In January 1966, I admitted that I was in love with her and had been for years, then asked if she would consider being my wife. She answered, 'Yes. Yes, I will!' Darlene was raised in the Seventh Day Adventist Church and there's no wedding ring involved in the engagement or marriage. The item considered practical was the wristwatch.

So, I gave her a Longines Wittnauer wristwatch, which back then was an expensive piece of jewelry. I had it engraved on the back and gave it to her as a form of us being formally engaged.

I must tell you that it would be years later in Nashville when I learned the fate of my friend from South Carolina. By chance, I ran into her father at a music Fan Fair and asked about her. The smile ran away from his face as he shared with me the truth. After I left South Carolina and married Darlene, she committed suicide. She was in love with me all along, and I never knew it. I just assumed she went on to marry the man she was engaged to and was alive and well. I sure was sorry to hear that and often wonder how different my life would be if I'd never read Pop's letter that day. You know, you wouldn't question the Ys in your life if you were content with the path you chose.

With a fiancé and wedding on the horizon, Allen set out to look for work. With his acquired skills, and military experience, it wasn't long before he was offered a very impressive job at Westinghouse Environmental Lab. Allen was hired as an engineer in the Underseas Division located in Baltimore, Maryland. He rented a nearby spare bedroom from an elderly couple so he could walk to work. The Underseas Division worked desperately to secure the contract for making the Navy's Mark 48 Torpedo. Allen's job was to oversee the entire lab with its testing of all the components that make up this weapon. He painstakingly took readings from mock underwater situations where environmental stressors such as heat, cold, shock, and vibration were recreated to evaluate its durability. It was critical that the torpedo was put through these tests to ensure success.

Although Allen thrived under pressure, and he could more than manage the intensity of his work, the sedentary nature of his desk job made him long for something different. He wanted more than anything to make a change in jobs and work for himself. First, he had to overcome numerous intimidating obstacles. Ironically, like the Mark 48 Torpedo, Allen had to withstand internal and external stressors, and develop the internal components to guarantee he wouldn't fail under any circumstance in life. Allen's mental strength and reliable coping mechanisms served him in overcoming what would normally be debilitating for most. Stressors such as adjusting to life back home, absorbing the ridicule for having served in Vietnam, battling Malaria, enduring the nightmares, and PTSD. Now he was under pressure to enter a life-long commitment with one person-a woman who would lean heavily upon him for fifty-one years to make it all happen for them both.

17

This Day of Days

*"Today you begin a journey together and your future will be
harmonious if you walk and work together. Each of you must do
his part and may you never take each other's love for granted."*
–Pastor Paul Cannon

With the wedding date set for August 21, 1966, Allen wanted
Darlene to meet his real father, and this time, he knew exactly
where to find him.

*My dad never stayed connected after we went out to the diner
that day. I wished he would have turned around and waved as
he walked back to the house, but he never did. Instead, he
turned and walked out of my life for a second time. When
Darlene and I were planning to get married, I really wanted
them to meet one another so we went to his house. I introduced
my bride-to-be, and he gave us a fifty-dollar bill and said,
'This is for your wedding. I can't be there because it would
be too complicated.' We were getting ready to leave and he
motioned for me to follow him upstairs. 'Allen, I want to show
you something.'*

*He entered a bedroom and twisted the doorstop, then moved
into another room and twisted that doorstop too. We entered a
third bedroom and followed the same procedure before walking
back into the hallway. I spotted a gun cabinet with its doors open
revealing a beautiful collection. Dad mechanically designed it
with wires going through the walls which opened the doors to*

this steel gun cabinet that would have otherwise taken dynamite to get open. He showed me the different guns in his collection, and it was wonderful. There was a twenty-five caliber, semi-automatic gun that he kept in a hollowed-out book. The pages were cut out of a book so that when the book was shut, it looked like a normal book. He placed that back on the shelf and I was watching all of this in awe, never realizing that his demonstration would prove to be important in the days to come. As I was leaving, he said, 'I want to get together again when you return from your honeymoon and start that father and son relationship we never had.' I replied, 'Oh my God, that would be wonderful!'

While still serving in Vietnam, Darlene forwarded the Seventh Day Adventist "Voice of Prophecy" course to Allen, which he promptly completed and returned. The fact that he did this course paved the way for him to be baptized into her church. This was necessary to have a Seventh-Day Adventist pastor marry them on August 21, 1966. The ceremony was held at Karl's Trinity Lutheran Church in Pottsville. The gorgeous white stone architecture and extensive stained-glass windows provided a picture-perfect setting for such a special occasion. The music was heavy with organ music echoing throughout, followed by the couple's chosen wedding song, 'This Day of Days,' by Jerry Vale. As the pastor began the ceremony, all eyes turned to the front and the attendees hushed to a whisper. In the background you heard the inevitable cries of a newborn baby that should have been left with a sitter. Pastor Cannon commences:

'Today you begin a journey together and your future will be harmonious if you walk and work together. Each of you must do his part and may you never take each other's love for granted. Allen may your strength be Darlene's protection; your character, her boast and pride. May your wife find in you that haven for

which the heart of a woman truly longs. Darlene, the Bible says Allen is the head of your new home and you should respect his judgments and continue to hold him in high esteem.'

Allen's voice was young and full of tenderness as he recited the vows to his bride.

I Allen, take thee Darlene to be my wedded wife and do promise to be thy loving and faithful husband. In plenty and in want, in joy and in sorrow, in sickness and in health, to love and to cherish, as long as we both shall live.

Newly Weds – August 21, 1966
Sitting in A.V. Tidmore's Cadillac

Married in the Lutheran Church
Karl Sterner belonged to

Darlene recited her vows without reservation because she was truly in love with Allen who had long ago swept her off her feet. She said, 'Yes!' to the idea that he was her person to be with in life, no matter what happens, and she wanted nothing more than to have at least six children with him. The wedding proved to be a wonderful celebration for all, except Darlene's mother, Laura. Her daughter Darlene meant everything to her, and she doted on her day in and day out. The two were inseparable and the realization that someone was taking her little girl away from her was just too much to bear. During the ceremony, Laura was so numbed up on nerve medication that it took two people to help her walk down the aisle and take her seat. Darlene's father congratulated his new son-in-law, but made it noticeably clear to Allen that moving Darlene away from them would absolutely kill Laura. No doubt Allen married the entire Haslam Clan when he married his fourth cousin, Darlene.

Along with a new wife came her parents and many other family members who would create a barrier between them. The first and only trip the couple would take alone throughout most of their marriage was a honeymoon in Bermuda. Even then, Darlene insisted on calling her mother to talk at great length every night from the honeymoon suite. It was this unhealthy codependency, and the fact that Darlene believed the Bible's command to honor thy mother and father before honoring her husband, that would eventually take its toll on their marriage.

Honeymoon in Bermuda
taken at the top of a lighthouse

Allen was anxious to finally pursue that father and son relationship that was ripped away from him. There were a multitude of questions teeming in Allen's head that had been gathering over the last twenty-two years. Now the answers he so desperately needed for healing and closure were just a day away, but unfortunately, that important day would never come.

We just returned from our honeymoon in Bermuda, and I was looking forward to getting together again with my dad. I believed that I would finally have the chance to ask him the questions I longed to have answered. We weren't home for more than a day when I received word from Florence that my dad had passed away at the early age of forty-nine. He died on August 29, 1966, from a massive heart attack. Any chance of knowing why my father left me, whether he truly wrote that goodbye letter to Pop, or any hope of reconnecting for that father and son relationship we never had, all died along with him. Jerry was supposed to come along with me to meet Karl that weekend for the very first time, and I felt so bad that he never got the chance. I remember standing next to Dad's coffin at the funeral with my brother beside me, looking down and seeing him lying there. Jerry was crying, 'I am sorry Dad, that I am seeing you like this for the first time.' I felt so bad for my brother and often wondered, for years after his death, if I may have caused it in some way. Maybe the stress of having me tapping on the door to be let back into his life was just too much for him. I would never get the answers I so desperately needed to resolve this aspect of my life. The day the man I idolized as a small child died, was the day a large part of me was lost too. The door leading to any chance at a loving father and son relationship slammed shut in my face. This time, it was one door I couldn't reopen and follow him through even if I wanted to.

After the funeral service, many of us went back to the house. I was standing downstairs with Florence and Darlene while one of my dad's closest friends was trying to get into the gun cabinet. He came down the stairs and asked Florence how to open it. She said, 'I don't know.' I spoke up and confessed that I knew how to get into it. They all looked at me in total amazement because how could I know that? I explained how my dad showed me before he died. I went upstairs and carefully went through the necessary steps. The gun cabinet opened, and everyone looked at me like I was the second coming. I am sure they were thinking, 'You've only been with your father a few times after all these years and he showed you, but we've been with him for over twenty years, and we didn't know!' A friend enquired, 'You know, your father promised me a twenty-five caliber semi-automatic-do you know where that would be?' I knew exactly where it was, and I pulled the book off the shelf and handed the gun to him. 'If my dad said you could have this, then it's yours.' I didn't want to be insulting, but I made it clear that the remaining guns now belonged to me.

Florence's sister threw a fit about all of this and so I hired an attorney who promptly went to the house to state that the guns legally belonged to me. According to New Jersey law, my brother and I should inherit no less than one-third of the house plus all its belongings.' Not surprising that Florence's sister wanted to fight this and threatened to get her own attorney. As Karl's biological son, I had the right to one-third of everything he owned including the house, but I only asked for what I thought was rightly mine-his gun collection. I reassured them, 'There's no need for you to waste your money on an attorney. I do want the guns, but I won't take anything else from you. There was no way I could take her house away from her, but I felt like my dad wanted me to have his gun collection because he only showed me how to access them. Of course, they agreed to this more than fair settlement, and in turn, I shared the collection with Jerry.

Although Allen's work ethic was superhuman at times, he was working under enormous pressure at the Westinghouse Environmental

Lab. A desk job was something he no longer wanted to do and without securing the hefty naval contract, the Underseas Division was doomed to close anyway. So, Allen took a leap of faith.

Darlene loved the way I left the house for work every day because I was always in a suit and tie, but the problem was that I couldn't sit at that desk and be that person any longer. I needed to get out and do other things. I spent three years writing calibration procedures for calibration equipment and the stress was enormous because Westinghouse was frantic to get this naval contract. The contract truly meant the survival of the entire Underseas Division and the fact they didn't get the contract, caused the entire plant to close within a year after I departed. The best part about working there was participating on the Westinghouse Rifle and Pistol Shooting Team. As the most accurate shooter, I was the anchor of the team, which meant when the competition was on the line, they relied on me to win it all for them. After I left Westinghouse, I worked several odd jobs to make ends meet while I was taking college classes. The first three years of our marriage were awful, because I had a difficult time adapting to being at home realizing that I was no longer in a war zone. I didn't want to see anyone because I didn't want to be labeled as crazy. Darlene was there for me and always trying to help, but I told her that I needed to be the one to fix this. I told her to be patient and just stick with me and I'd be okay, but we had a shaky start.

I thought it might be helpful if I concentrated on helping others in some way, so I spoke candidly with the pastor of our Baltimore First Church. I explained to him that I wanted to volunteer my time and be more involved. He said, 'You know, we need a good Pathfinder leader for our youth.' I had no idea what that position entailed, but I volunteered for it, leading thirty-five children ages eight to fourteen years old. I wanted to do something positive with the group, so we started collecting food for the needy. I didn't think it would happen, but I reached out to the President of the Chesapeake Conference and asked if one of the vacant buildings located on the campgrounds could be designated as a clubhouse for our group. With his permission, we now had our very own clubhouse to operate out of and we called ourselves the Schipperkes (Pronounced SKIP-per-keys). We did all sorts of fun and wonderful things like various crafts and gathering money and food for the poor.

I led big camping trips, and I showed them survival techniques and how to cook without cookware. We used coat hangers and aluminum foil to make our pots and pans. We had beautiful camping trips to Blue Mountain, but we had terrible rainstorms in the middle of the trips. Kids would be running out of their tents while my leaking tent had a running stream down the middle of it. We packed the kids into cars because that was the only way to keep them dry and took all the sleeping bags to laundromats. Yep, we were having fun. I got close to a lot of the kids as some of them were coming from broken homes and needed guidance. I also needed to play the "Dad" part, watching out for certain guys trying to talk to girls behind the tents because their hormones at that age were working overtime. I was their leader for four years in a row and together we accomplished so much.

It was during Allen's fourth year as the group's leader when he came to realize God's reason for having him there all along.

As we always did, the group gathered food at Thanksgiving time. We collected all kinds of canned goods; boxes of cereal and the annex tables were all filled with food to deliver. The night before Thanksgiving, we were supposed to go to the annex to individually box up everything for delivery to the families needing it most. The morning news called for a slight ten percent chance of rain, and I said to Darlene, 'You know, I can't have the kids delivering food in the rain.' Darlene questioned my decision, 'It's only a ten percent chance of rain.' I said, 'Nah, I am going to cancel it today, and we will do it another time.' I called the adult counselors to relate my decision and they all gave me a hard time about it. I finally said, 'Look guys, I am cancelling the meeting tonight and that is that.' I was the leader, so it was my call to make, and I made it.

I'll never forget, one of our counselors called me that night around seven thirty and his voice was clearly shaken. He asked, 'Have you heard? The annex blew up! The gas furnace underneath it exploded and the annex along with part of the church were destroyed. We rushed to the church and of course, there were fire trucks, police, news vans, and commotion. The scene was surreal, and as soon as we were able to get close enough to look in, we noticed the concrete floors of the annex were entirely gone. The walls were blown out in the exact same spot where thirty-five kids and adult counselors would have been sorting food. I was in total shock, but overjoyed that God used me to save those children. I have no doubt in my mind that God worked through me because nobody else would have cancelled that meeting over a slight chance of rain. As they say, our Lord works in mysterious ways, and this was a real revelation for me. The parents saw me in church and thanked me and calls came in thanking me for what I did. I said, 'Well, it wasn't me. I had nothing to do with it. God used me to make that call.'

For the first time in my life, I engaged in something beyond myself and my past. I pushed myself to do more for other people and that took my mind off all that I had been through and that's how I managed to get past it. You can't just dwell on your problems because there's so many other people that have problems too. Once you concentrate on helping others, it helps you in return. That's how I've done it all my life. To anyone out there who has problems, just concentrate on others, and do what you can to help them make their lives better and then you will truly heal yourself.

Allen was beginning to heal but was still deeply troubled over killing the school children and the young Viet Cong soldier. Before becoming involved in the church, he never talked to anyone about what happened in Vietnam. It was in church where he felt comfortable enough to confide in a pastor because deep down, he wanted to know why it happened the way it did. It was a split-second decision that night, but he could never understand why it had to be the young soldier who died instead of him.

When it comes to a split-second chance of which person dies, I want to know who flipped that coin. Was it God? Under those circumstances, you have to ask why? I asked my pastor, 'Why did the young soldier have to die?' The minister didn't have the answer, but he told me that when I get to heaven, I'll need to ask God directly. Only God will have the answer and that's what I had to live with but talking openly about what happened really helped me.

Allen was healing and constructing a productive and positive life one piece at a time with the help of Darlene's love, the church, and the Pathfinders. Allen tried keeping Darlene as close to her mother and father as possible by making an offer to purchase a lot close to the village of Wadesville where she grew up. This village where Darlene lived until she was twenty-three was pretty in its day, and she and Allen shared fond memories of being there together as children. It seemed like a natural first step to build a home and life thereafter they were married. In hindsight, it was lucky that their offer fell through. The loving, young couple was destined for something better: a family of their own and a future rich with opportunities in Ellicott City, Maryland. Allen was an ambitious person, working best under pressure. Now, with the support of Darlene, the enterprising man was about to take the world by storm.

18

No Quit Inside of Me

*"No one will ever fully be able to understand the internal battles you
had to endure just to make it here today. Be proud of the way you
fought to save yourself. Be proud of the way you survived."*
–Bianca Sparacino

After three years of marriage and a tumultuous transitional
period for Allen, Darlene was thrilled to learn that she was
pregnant with the couple's first child. Being like a big kid herself,
Darlene loved playing with and teaching children in the church and
dreamed of having at least six kids of her own. For Allen, as the sole
provider for his family, the discovery of another life entering his,
brought a heightened sense of responsibility and an immense
pressure to make it all happen for his family. Much like a carbon
atom, Allen could endure intense pressure and emerge a brilliant and
sparkling diamond because he worked tirelessly to overcome any of
life's challenges.

He temporarily put aside his musical endeavors and shifted his
focus to raising a family, buying a home, and setting the foundations
to secure a strong future. In April of 1969, Allen and Darlene left their
apartment and purchased their first Cape Cod style home together
in Ellicott City. The price of the home was fourteen thousand nine
hundred dollars and they needed to qualify. The young couple solicited
the help of their old friend, A.V. Tidmore who was kind enough to
loan five thousand dollars for a down payment. At the same time,
Allen attended Catonsville Community College and College Park
Main Campus at the University of Maryland, working towards a

degree in Industrial Management with a minor in Labor Relations. He burned the candle at both ends going to school, remodeling the house, and working part-time at a company called, Joy Camper. Allen always pushed himself to take on more than ever. His course load was eighteen credit hours one semester and nineteen hours the second semester and he was staying up all hours of the night completing assignments and reports.

During the week, Allen also worked part-time as a Carpenter's Foreman building cabinets and designing the interiors of mobile camper vans. It was his job to utilize every square inch of interior space, guided by the customer's drawings, to turn dreams into reality. On September 25, 1969, the couple was blessed with a beautiful baby girl they named Janelle Darlene Sterner. Allen was in the thick of a full life with a wife, newborn baby, an insanely heavy college course load, as well as a demanding part-time job. Just as life was moving onward and upward, a call from the past rang in.

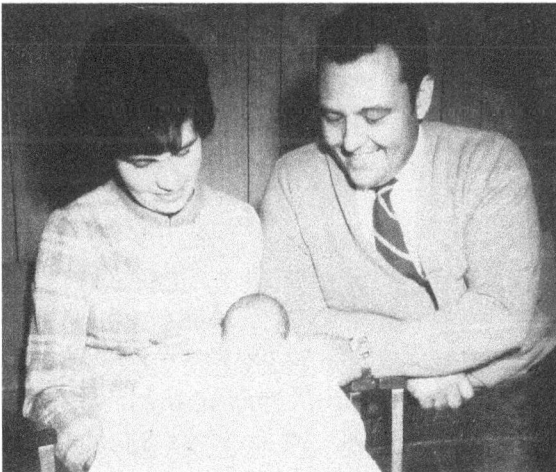

Proud parents with Janelle

The phone rang one evening and Darlene answered it. The person on the other end hung the phone up on her. A brief time later, the phone rang again, and a woman asked Darlene if she was my wife. That woman was the mother of the girl I dated throughout my service in Japan. She was the first caller who hung up the phone when Darlene answered. I took the phone, and her mother asked if I realized that her daughter was still wearing my ring? Then my ex-fiancé got on the phone and said to me, 'I didn't know you were married.' I replied, 'Yes, I am married, and we have a little girl.' She said, 'Well, I have a little girl too, and I am not married.' She was insinuated that I should leave Darlene and my daughter to marry her and have her daughter instead. Of course, I told her that I couldn't do that and reminded her that we had agreed long ago that we were done. She wasn't done, and it wasn't over for her because she claimed she was still in love with me. It didn't matter because for me, it was over.

Fifteen months following the birth of Janelle, Allen was thrilled to learn his family was growing when Darlene announced that she was pregnant once again. The superstition she believed, stating that you couldn't get pregnant while nursing, wasn't true. With a second baby on the way, Allen realized that their house also needed to be enlarged. He devised a unique way to raise the roof and add on more bedrooms.

Our first house was a little, two-bedroom Cape Cod in Ellicott City. When we bought it in 1969, there was no upstairs, so I decided to raise the roof and put two more bedrooms and a bathroom up there. With the help of my friend and expert carpenter, Jerry Carlson, we took a very unconventional approach and began the renovation. Jerry was one of my best friends and he moved in with us just to help me with this enormous project. In fact, the expansion would have been impossible to manage without his assistance. We began by cutting down the eaves of the roof starting at the peak. Not wanting to completely tear off the roof, we simply pulled all the nails out and jacked it up with railroad jacks and built walls around it with windows. Next, we set the roof down onto the new, eight-foot-high walls and reattached it. It really worked out great and now we had plenty of space for our growing family.

Nineteen seventy-one proved to be a banner year for Allen with the birth of his only son, Travis Allen Sterner on the first of October. It was also the year he brought to life his first entrepreneurial idea he named "Pretti-Pet." With his wife's support, along with his experience converting vans into living space at Joy Camper, Allen pressed forward with the idea to convert vans into a mobile pet grooming salon. These custom mobile salons were equipped with every tool needed to deliver a top-notch grooming experience and could be conveniently parked in the driveway of each customer. This aspect alleviated the need to drop off your pet with the groomer, wait for several hours, then drive all the way back to pick them up. A Pretti-Pet grooming van traveled directly to the client's location and completed the job on-site. This innovative idea was the first of its kind anywhere East of the Mississippi and it caught on fast.

Travis and Janelle standing next to the Pretti-Pet Mobile Salon

With Allen's knack for design and his superior carpentry skills, he designed and built the vans, complete with a hot water source for bathing. Water was heated via a propane tank and gray water emptied into a stainless-steel holding tank below. The design included a state-of-the-art grooming table and an area where the dog could relax as they dried. True to his trade, every inch of the van interior was maximized. Allen was the company's first groomer and remarkably he was self-taught. An eight-week grooming course in New York was a consideration, but at the tune of eleven hundred dollars, it was out of the question. With his insistence on perfection, Allen quickly became accomplished at grooming all breeds of dogs and even a few cats.

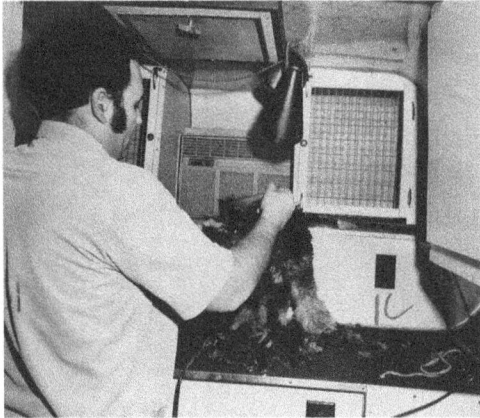

Allen as the first groomer of Pretti-Pet

He didn't quit until the customer was more than thrilled with the results. Prices were reasonable and competitive with a basic groom starting off at thirteen dollars and optional add-ons such as anti-flea dips, nail trimming, and teeth brushing were available. House calls cost three dollars more than visiting the groomer in a set location, but customers thought the convenience was well worth it. Numerous local newspaper articles were written about the novel approach and people jumped at the chance to use the service. In fact, people would see the van driving around town and make appointments through the window of the van at stop lights, or while Allen was parked for lunch. People caught on to the idea and hired Allen to design a van for their hair styling business as well. "Hair-A-Van" was created, and the complete conversion of the mobile hair salon took Allen five months and fifteen thousand dollars, but it was an enormous success.

Once up and running, he turned the company over to Darlene who dispatched groomers, set appointments, and studied maps so she could hand write driving directions to and from each customer's location. She was an absolute natural for the position having received her associate degree in Secretarial Arts, Short-Hand, and Typewriting. Darlene was gifted and could type close to a hundred words per minute and handwrite information as fast as you could say it. She had previous secretarial experience too, having worked for the Chesapeake Conference for the Seventh Day Adventist Church. For six months, she also worked as a secretary for the radio evangelist, Pastor Joe Cruze, and with her deep knowledge of the Bible, she wrote many of his speeches. The pastor was an incredibly good man and Allen thought the world of him. Pastor Cruze relied heavily upon Allen's expertise to keep the radio equipment running properly. Many times, often into the early hours of the morning, Allen could be found at the station working under the pastor's desk trouble-shooting radio equipment so that the radio show could air later that morning without a hitch.

From 1971 until 2018 we did very well with the mobile grooming business. At the time I sold it in 2018, the business had grown to five vans on the road with six full-time groomers, and over twenty thousand regular clients. We tracked our client's information manually, writing on five by seven index cards that we stored in the office. We started at thirteen dollars for basic grooming, and by 2018, we were getting sixty-five dollars per dog.

Despite being saturated with Pretti-Pet, college courses, two young children, and working full-time at Joy Camper Company, Allen jumped at an unexpected business opportunity. Ms. Atchley was the sweet lady who owned the Joy Camper Company. After years in the business, she was ready to retire and was looking for the exactly right person to take it over. Of course, her ambitious Carpenter's Foreman would be the perfect fit to buy her out.

We had our Cape Cod house for just over three years when we learned that my boss, Ms. Atchley, was going to sell her Joy Camper Company. Out of curiosity, I asked her what she wanted for it, and she shared that they wanted to get fifteen thousand dollars, which included the space, tools, and materials. I thought that I could really make a go of this business, so we took a huge leap of faith. We put a second mortgage on our home and bought the camper company in early May of 1972, renaming it, Travel Van Camper.

This was a scary step because we were barely getting by, watching, and recording every single penny spent, and this acquisition meant that everything was going to escalate with our mortgage payment. By that time, we had two children and I had invested everything into it. Our motto was, 'If you can draw it, I can build it.' All the work that we did was in-house including the leather-like upholstery. I had a tailor/secretary named Margaret who had her own office at the company, and we set up an industrial sewing machine for her to use just down the hall. She sewed all the beads that went around the cushions with a heavy cord. She was very loyal and promptly made me aware of anyone trying to take advantage of me in business. In total, I had nine people working for me and we were really doing well until June 14, 1972, when hurricane Agnes hit.

I had just enough time after buying the business to fully stock the building with tools, materials, and camper vans before we were dealt a devastating blow. The river ran right next to the building where I housed the business in Laurel, Maryland and the flood caused by Hurricane Agnes took the entire thing out. I mean, I lost it all, my tools, all the product, and the campers. Every single supply floated down the river. Against the warning of the emergency responders, I hopped into a canoe and tried to recover as much as I could, but it was a total loss. It was so disheartening because everything I worked for was gone and I didn't have the insurance to cover anything. We were poor, and Darlene was raising the kids and busy running Pretti-Pet and we needed to get back into it somehow. So, I applied for a one percent governmental loan and luckily, they granted it and I worked myself back into business.

Business was once again going very well, and my company won first place at the prestigious "Vantasia." This was a large, annual show of all the van conversion companies along the East Coast, so it was a big deal. Out of hundreds of vans brought in for the competition, we won first place for 'Best Design.' We took home a large trophy and of course the bragging rights that came along with it. We capitalized on that win, advertising the fact that we were number one and it drew in even more business. We were thriving and completing all sorts of camper van conversions. In fact, between 1972-1978, my company successfully converted over thirty-five hundred vans. I was fully recovered from hurricane Agnes when the next large hurricane, Eloise, arrived in 1975. I lost everything all over again and still didn't have the flood insurance because it wasn't available in our area. I couldn't let that stop me, so I rebuilt the business from scratch all over again.

For a few years after being wiped out a second time, my business continued to do well until 1978 when the gasoline crisis hit. That's when lines to buy gas were all over the place

*and people weren't buying campers because it required too much
fuel to fill the tank and it became too expensive to drive them.
As a result, I sold Travel Van Camper in late 1978 and went
full-time into construction and focused again on my music. All
this time, I was recording in Maryland and signed with Sundial
Records in Nashville from 1975-1977. In 1978, I signed with a
label out of New York called Century Artist Records. My producer
back then was Doug Arthur who wrote the song, 'I'm Gonna
Buy Me a Camel.' Doug knew of this record label in New York,
and they were interested in having me record it. I signed and
recorded the song, and on the flipside of the record they put a
song I wrote called; 'I am No Good Without You.' The record label
pushed and promoted it to the point of national recognition. I was
steadily moving up in the charts, neck-and-neck with Jerry Reed's
hit called, 'Who Put the Line in Gasoline?' Jerry topped higher
on the charts than I did, but the fact that we were in the radio
charts at the same time meant a lot to me. Although we never met
in person, Jerry Reed was someone I admired and respected
because he was not only a good singer, but also a tremendous
lead guitar player.*

From the time Travis was born in 1971 until 1978, there was a
tremendous amount happening and the couple was experiencing
marital trouble. Allen had no idea at that time that Darlene was
pregnant with their third child, but ultimately a baby would help to
bring the couple closer. Rebecca Lynn Sterner was born on August
22, 1978. Rebecca was a name in the Bible that Darlene loved, and
Lynn was in honor of Allen's brother, Jerry Lynn Sterner. Altogether,
the year marked another milestone for Allen with the selling of Travel
Van Camper, a recording contract with Century Artists Records in
New York, the birth of their daughter, and in February, the purchase
of a historical farm outside of Ellicott City. They weren't sure if they

could afford such a large place with Allen recently out of work, but the thirty-acre farm on Johnnycake Road was an incredibly special place. No doubt, the home was meant for this family who filled its walls with love from the minute they moved in. This farm would become a favorite gathering spot for friends and family throughout the years and provide the optimal place to raise children and continue to break the cycle of abuse.

19

There's No Place Like Home
N39° 18'54.8" W76° 47' 4.3"

"A rare beauty, our farm was always my haven and a piece of heaven secretly stored on earth, with its own secret coordinates."
—Janelle Sterner

Johnnycake Road farmhouse in Windsor Mill, Maryland

"This afternoon we have come into the house of God to lay the foundation of a new Christian home that under *His* guidance, shall last forever. This union is to form the nucleus of a new home which shall be a miniature heaven on earth. A little heaven, to go to heaven in. In the hope and with the prayer that it may be so for you." These are the words that Pastor Paul Cannon spoke to Darlene and Allen during their wedding ceremony and now, years later, they were set to create their miniature heaven on earth. At least it seemed that way to his wife and children, but for Allen the farm was a heavy load to bear. The blood, sweat, and tears he poured into that farm was a true labor of love and the improvements he made over the following forty years, may still be standing decades after he is gone from this earth.

Becky was born in August of 1978, and we bought the farm earlier that year in February, after Darlene noticed a property For Sale sign on Johnnycake Road. We were looking for land to build a home on and the location was ideal, so we didn't waste any time in going to see it. The head of the house, Ms. Smith was also acting as the real estate agent. She was very congenial and when we asked her where the property for sale was, she replied with a proud grin, 'You're standing on it and it includes everything here. It's thirty acres!' It was so beautiful at the time; we didn't dare dream of affording it and thought we were way over our heads looking at this one. The thirty-acre property included a historical, 1840s era farmhouse, a barn built during the Civil War, various outbuildings, swimming pool, mature woods, creek, and peaceful surroundings filled with wildlife. I said, 'Wow, I can't imagine that we can afford this.' But she offered an encouraging nudge and replied, 'All you need to do is put in a contract and tell me what it is that you want. I am asking one hundred and eighty-nine thousand dollars.' It was just beautiful, and I thought, 'Okay, let's do this!'

We had the property appraised and it came back at one hundred and seventy thousand dollars, and that's the offer I made in the contract. It was so bewildering, and I don't think I could even do this today, because at the time, I didn't have a job. I had just sold the Travel Van Camper business and Pretti-Pet was still in its infant stages, not exactly a thriving business at the time. We were really struggling, but the Laurel Savings and Loan Bank gave us the mortgage anyway. As a down payment, we sold our starter home for fifty thousand dollars which was just over a thirty-five-thousand-dollar profit in nine years. Now we had the mortgage payment of nine hundred dollars, and it was hard to come up with that each month, but somehow, we did. Just making the mortgage was a monthly challenge, but then we were hit with unexpected expenses on top of that. Within a year of buying the property, our entire water system went out and forced us to install a five-hundred-dollar submersible pump. Just weeks later, the hot water heater quit working and with three kids at the time, it was tough to make ends meet. Sometimes life would get me down.

Darlene's belief in God was strong, and she told me not to get down or depressed in life. To her, depression was a sin because God didn't want that for you. So, despite all of life's pressures, I could never let Darlene catch me feeling down or depressed. Sometimes, at all hours of the night, I'd play my guitar and write songs. I'd be in my bedroom, and she'd be downstairs with the kids. I sat with the lights off, just listening to the sound of my guitar-strumming and producing melodies. The sound of the guitar in the darkness of a room was pure therapy for me. If I felt the least bit down or worried about something, I'd do that for an hour or so, come back downstairs to play with the kids, and everything was fine. That guitar in a dark room gave me something unbelievable; hitting every string, one right after the other, and I still do that to this day. The chords ring out in the darkness better than they do in the light. It's a strange thing, but that's the way it happened with me, and I loved that because it was a dear friend. The guitar, unlike people, never let me down.

"The Kiss" – Allen referred to Darlene as his Ali MacGraw

Darlene's parents Laura and Fred Williams spent the last twelve years begrudging the fact that Allen married their precious daughter and moved her away from their home. Darlene spent every weekend at her parents in Pennsylvania and often her mother came to the farm for extended stays. When they were apart, Laura and Darlene shared lengthy phone conversations every night. With so much happening in her daughter's life by 1978, it wasn't hard for Laura to convince herself that she was needed. After thirty-five years of teaching Business, Typing, and Shorthand at the high school, Fred retired. Laura was a homemaker so now they were both free to move anywhere in the world, and they set their sights on Johnnycake Road. The summer before Becky was born, Allen's in-laws moved in for life.

As a single family everything was working out fine and now the farmhouse bulged with four adults and three children. Laura was no doubt some help to Darlene, and the kids seemed to enjoy having their grandparents around. However, for Allen, having his in-laws living under the same roof marked the beginning of losing the loving and close relationship he once enjoyed with his wife. There was more love between Darlene and Allen when it was just the two of them, but now, mother and daughter were inseparable. The two of them spent every minute together, even joining each other in the bathroom to talk at great length, and often shared the same sleeping arrangements, edging Allen out of the picture altogether.

From that moment on, Allen and Darlene never shared a vacation or so much as an outing alone. Allen became the modern-day "Ward Bond," leading the family excursions in an RV. As the only person willing to drive that large of a vehicle, Allen chalked up over ten thousand miles in just three weeks driving the entire family to visit various destinations. It was entirely up to Allen to get everyone back home safely and in time for work, so he slept instead of sight-seeing and drove through the night. Everywhere he and Darlene went, the whole clan had to go too, and that was draining. On top of it, Fred offered no help whatsoever.

Fred was known to do nothing, was often found reading in bed, and never lifted a finger to help me. He never cooked, washed dishes, or put on a load of laundry. On family outings, he insisted on wearing his three-piece suit, complete with a business hat, which made him look like he was dropped into the middle of the scene straight out of Mars. While visiting Sarasota Beach, Florida, Fred strolled along the sand in his dress shoes, suit, and hat, while beachgoers ran past him in their swimsuits. He was the type of person people made fun of because of these quirks. While teaching, he was the favorite target of student pranks; often having his keys or hat stolen from his desk. Fred stood out in a group of guys and came across as uncoordinated and weak. The teasing and torment he endured made him physically ill with a nervous condition forcing an early retirement. Fred left his profession just short of his thirty-five-year mark, so the local Board of Education denied him his full pension. However, the school system failed to credit him with his accrued unused sick leave, and I just couldn't let it go unchallenged.

I called a meeting with the Board of Education, dressed up in a professional looking three-piece suit, and with briefcase in hand, went to secure that full pension for Fred. I entered the room with confidence, put my briefcase down at the head of the table, opened it, and stood there looking at each one of the board members. I began by announcing that I was Fred Williams' counselor from Baltimore and asked, 'How are we going to settle this?' I never once used the word attorney or lawyer, and I explained that Fred had enough vacation days built up over his career to earn his full pension even if he quit right now. I asked again, 'How far do you want to take this? Or you can decide right now to give it to him as he deserves.' The board asked me to leave the room while they discussed the matter privately. After a short wait, their decision was to grant Fred his full pension without a fight. I smiled and slightly nodded, 'Gentleman, you've made a good decision here. Thank you very much.' I returned to my car where Laura lay in hiding on the floor of the backseat. She nervously asked, 'Oh Allen, what happened?' I told her the board's decision, and she began to cry. Fred lived to be eighty-five-years old receiving his full pension, and after he passed away, Laura continued to draw a percentage until her death at ninety-seven. All because of this one meeting and of course, Darlene was thrilled with me for pulling this off.

Allen was working harder than ever to maintain the farm, pay bills, and give his children the lifestyle he always dreamed of having himself. To accomplish this, he never stopped trying to find ways to make more money. In 1979, Allen started the A.K. Sterner Construction Company, LLC and hired employees to work alongside him on projects. Allen was a doer and loved to be in the thick of every project.

When I worked in the construction business, I enjoyed getting in there with my guys and building things. It was always my opinion that they needed to see me doing things as opposed to just being the person that tells them what to do. I always told my guys that I would never ask them to do anything that I have not already done myself. When roofing, I've been on the highest peaks of the roof, tied off, and laying shingles right along-side of them. That was the difference, and I really enjoyed the work. I still have both my general contractor's and home improvement licenses to this day and throughout the history of my company, we built and refurbished over eight thousand apartments in eleven different complexes. The world just wasn't big enough for me. I needed so much more, and I couldn't stand to do just one thing because my mind couldn't do just one thing. At night I could put it all together in my head. I'd lay in bed, and I could see all the lumber come together and how it had to fasten and my mind simply couldn't rest. To this day, I push myself to do more and be more. It seemed like there was always so much that I needed to do, but I wasn't sure what that was. I just knew that I had to keep moving forward, working hard, and creating good things. For me, there never was, nor will there ever be a finish line.

Allen delighted in the work he did to improve the farm in every way imaginable. He built a playground area, refurbished the swimming pool, built a luxury two-bedroom apartment above the barn, planted flowers, hand-dug and set over three hundred fence posts, installed four board fence rails, erected sturdy rock retaining walls, remodeled the interior of the main house, created a home office, and more. With each project, Allen held a deep appreciation for the hands that worked on that farm generations before him. He especially admired the primary stone wall holding up his 1860s era barn. It was fun to imagine the hardworking men of the past carefully placing each stone, never realizing it would still be standing years later. Allen himself was crafty and sharp, and he too constructed objects on that farm that would withstand the hands of time. However, his marriage was not one of them. Despite his time and efforts, Allen's relationship with Darlene began to crumble and he found himself spending more time away from home with his band than he did with his own family.

Allen's Canyon River Band

I had dependable project managers to oversee the construction projects while I was gone, so I could be on the road for a week or two at a time-playing gigs with my Canyon River Band. Back then we got some decent pay working in the clubs and my band and I were like family. We laughed and had such a wonderful time performing together, and the crowds loved us. The Canyon River Band stayed together through the 1980s and a good part of the 1990s and all throughout the years, we were on the road a lot. When I was on the road for extended periods of time, Janelle asked Darlene if she missed me, and if my being gone bothered her. She answered, 'No. Your dad needs to do this because his music keeps him from getting old.' She knew I always came home to be there for her, and the family whenever she needed me, so she supported my absence in her own way. For years, Darlene was always with her mother and never came to watch a single show of mine. It wasn't until after her mother passed away in 2002 at the age of ninety-seven, that she could be seen sitting in the audience.

Allen was strong minded and that is no doubt one of the reasons he endured so much pain in life and still managed to succeed. There has never been any quit in Allen, except for one instance when quitting was the smartest thing to do.

I smoked when I went into the Air Force and continued until 1980 before I finally quit. I was doing an intimate show with just me and my guitar for a week in Chicago. They put me up in a one-bedroom apartment and I was waiting there until it was showtime. The organizers came over to tell me they were ready for me, but first I needed a smoke. I asked the guy if he had one on him, but he didn't. There was no time to run out and get one, but I sure needed a cigarette. I only needed one, so I emptied the trash can in the kitchen and spread out the trash all over the floor. Even just a butt that I could light and get a couple of drags off. I couldn't find one and kept looking desperately through the garbage. Suddenly, the image of myself came to me as if I were sitting on top of the refrigerator looking down at this absurd scene. I was so ashamed and thought, 'If the people over there that I am about to entertain could see me now, they would walk away.' I just felt so ashamed, 'Dear God, never again am I going to let a cigarette dictate to me and put me on my hands and knees sifting through garbage to find something on which I can puff. I'll never be a slave to a cigarette ever again.' From that moment on, I never picked up another cigarette and over-powered any feelings that I had to smoke. I walked over and did that show and I felt fine. It was just mind over matter and I quit cold turkey that very minute.

Allen didn't want to quit his marriage cold turkey, although it was much more than a simple situation of mind over matter. Allen couldn't deny feeling unloved, unappreciated, and lonely. The marriage had hit its twelve-year anniversary and working all day, coming home late, heating up his own leftovers, doing his own laundry, arguing with his wife, and often sleeping separate from her, was unraveling any remaining closeness he felt. For things to get better, sometimes they first must get worse. However, once you make the turn, the homestretch can be a grand show of mighty stamina and a big-hearted effort to make it work. The key is sticking together in plenty and in want, in joy and in sorrow, in sickness and in health, and to love and to cherish each other as long as you both shall live.

20

You Get What You Resist

"If you ever get the chance to treat them the way they treated you,
I hope you choose to walk away and do better."
–Najwa Zebian

Kitty told Allen she wished he would have come back from Vietnam a paraplegic so he could never leave her again. Contrary to what you might think, leaving his mother behind wasn't as easy for Allen as it should have been. Dying alone was Kitty's ultimate fear, and when she could no longer exercise control over her boys, she parasitically latched on to whomever she could. Of course, she slathered the guilt on thick all along the way.

Jerry reflects:

We retaliated against our mother when we reached the point where we just didn't care anymore. We wanted nothing to do with her and we were old enough that we could just take off and go. Just before my twenty-first birthday, I got a 1949 Plymouth, and went off to college in Wilmington, Delaware to attend business school. From there, I was drafted into the Army. Personally, I gave Mom no consideration, whatsoever. We were older and she couldn't dominate us near what she did before, unless she beat us to a point where our brains were scrambled, and we didn't know any better. We should have had severe brain damage as many times as we were hit. I just stated that I was going out with this person or with that person and told her to get Nana to come over and stay, or whatever. She pleaded with me, 'No, no! Don't leave me!' I insisted, 'I'm sorry, but we're going. Goodbye.' On our way out the door, she would always say, 'Jerry, you can have all the girlfriends you want, but there's no one in this world that's gonna be any better to you than your mother.' She tried convincing us while growing up that she was all we would ever need and kept reiterating this from elementary to high school. I can still hear her now, 'Nobody's gonna be to you what your mother has been; always stick with you, always be there for you. Nobody else will be as loyal and faithful to you, as your own mother.'

When Allen finished his service in the Air Force, he received an Honorable Discharge and was given thirteen thousand dollars. With a fiancé and a new life to start, God knows he could have really used that money to get ahead. Instead, Allen used it to keep the roof over his mother's head. When Kitty was kicked out of Annie's, Pop put the family up at 1504 A (which today is 1506) West Norwegian Street in Pottsville where she continued to live until the day she died. Once both of her parents were gone, Kitty clung to others for financial and emotional support and Allen felt as if he had to fill his grandfather's shoes.

To keep Mom in the house that Pop provided for her at 1504 A West Norwegian Street, I had to pay a percentage of the back-dated state assistance money she owed. I know Darlene didn't understand my reasoning, mainly because we could have used my Air Force discharge pay to eventually buy a home of our own. The thing was, my mom was never self-sustaining a day in her life, and I knew she'd always need my assistance. Nana was as dumb as she was mean. She never wrote out a check, grocery shopped, and didn't know a thing about living alone. Pop was aware of this and in the event of his death, he wanted to make sure that 1504A went to Nana first and then to Kitty.

The apartment house with the beauty parlor on the ground level at 1215 Market Street had previously been sold just prior to Pop passing away in November of 1971. Pop phoned me wanting to talk in person and I suggested we do so when I came for Thanksgiving just a few days away. Unfortunately, that day never came because he died before we had that conversation and as I look back now, I am sure he wanted to talk about whether Mom should ever own her own place. He had little faith in her ability to keep up a home and wanted me to take it over. The night he died he and Nana got into a very distressing argument, and he called his daughter, Jeanette, to tell her about it. He went to bed that night with a troubled mind, and never saw the light of morning, dying in his sleep from a stroke at the age of seventy-eight. It's horrible how people get greedy when a loved one passes away, but Aunt Doris called to get me up there to Pop's house as soon as possible. Pop's belongings were disappearing fast and the only possessions I really wanted were his desk and the mandolin that he treasured.

After Pop died, Nana moved in with Kitty at 1504 A West Norwegian Street and stayed with her until she passed away on March 31, 1976, from complications of pneumonia. Once again, Kitty hesitated to call a doctor when her mother first took ill, and the result was deadly. With both parents now deceased, Kitty leaned on Allen more than ever to take care of her, and he did. Allen paid every one of her expenses despite the burden of his own financial commitments. Kitty married her fourth husband, William (Bill) Goho and Allen hosted the wedding ceremony at his farm. Bill was a renowned chef in New York City at one time and a wonderful man. It's not clear what he saw in Kitty, but it's tragic that he spent the last years of his life ensnared in her web of abuse.

After a couple of years of marriage, Bill was diagnosed with Parkinson's, which caused him to posture; meaning he freezes up and is unable to move. Mom assaulted that poor man believing it might snap him out of his posturing. Frozen and defenseless, he withstood her pouncing on him mercilessly for losing his bowels. We began noticing a change in Bill's outgoing personality, and multiple bruises on his body. Of course, I immediately suspected my mom and knew we had to do something. We secretly placed a recorder under Bill's chair, turned it on, and left it there. He was fine when we left and after a few hours we returned to listen to the recording.

As suspected, we captured the sounds of Mom shouting at him and I cringed when we heard those distinctive whacks. I played the recorded evidence back and offered Mom an ultimatum. Either we were taking Bill out of there, or I was going to call the police and let them take him, but either way, he was leaving her that day. She didn't want the police called, so we removed him ourselves. She was frantic and insisting on knowing where we were taking him, but we never would say. Bill was so willing to go with us because he knew he'd finally be free. He was pointing to things he wanted to take with him, and we snatched them up and packed it all in the car. We placed him in an undisclosed assisted living center, and it was like watching an animal being set free and running off into the woods. Bill was a pleasant guy, and everybody loved him in the nursing center. We visited him every chance we got, and the nurses smiled when they told us, 'We think he has a girlfriend living in such and such a room.' It warmed our hearts to know he was doing so well.

With Bill removed from her house, Kitty took in a roommate to help with expenses and to keep her company. The layout of the house provided a separate living space on the bottom floor, with its own exclusive access. A lady by the name of Mary Ellen and her daughter occupied it, but the place overall was in disrepair and filthy. It's not surprising that the two women had something going on between them and it was, yet another unhealthy situation Kitty manufactured. Despite the craziness, Allen stayed in touch with his mother and continued to pay her bills until the day she died.

My Uncle Cecil called me and said, 'I have some sad news. We found your mom, and she passed away from congestive heart failure.' As mean and ruthless as my mom was to me, I had been paying all her bills every month. She had this terrible phone bill from talking to her naturalist doctor in California. You know, my mom never once commented on how successful I was, it was always about what I could do for her. I paid off her debt and only then would she say, 'Thank you.' To hear anything close to that, my actions had to be related to helping her in some way. After I received the outrageous telephone bill, I called and was very ugly to her. We couldn't afford to pay those bills to begin with, and it seemed like she didn't care about that. Whether we could afford them or not was not important to her, but she knew we had to pay them because she couldn't. I insisted that her running up the bills had to stop. Hateful isn't the right word, but I wasn't loving to her. I've always felt bad about that because she started to cry on the phone and I said, 'Okay, just forget it!' I wasn't nice enough in the way that you should be if you were aware that your mom was going to die that night. Of course, I didn't know that.

You know, over the years, people have told me, 'Well, the way you've been treated, why should you feel guilty about that?' It didn't matter, because I will always feel guilty that I ended the telephone conversation without saying, 'I love you, Mom.' I did love her, but the problem was, she never loved me. That's something I live with, but who doesn't love their mother? Anyway, I know I tried to love her, but then again, I don't know if it was me trying to love her or me trying to save my own life. I did things to please her, but was it so I could survive? I truthfully forgave my mom a long time ago and my feeling towards her is not hatred, but sadness.

Last known photo of Kitty with Allen Circa 1989

I feel deprived that I never had a loving mother. Everyone wants to have a good mother, and I didn't have one. I had a person who didn't love, appreciate, or even care about me in so many ways. I feel bad for her because she had a son that would have loved her unconditionally and she threw all that away. I would have loved her with all my heart, and I needed to love her, but her sickness prevented that. She lost just as much as I did, and I feel badly. I couldn't stop it and I had no way to prevent it, so I guess we both had to live through it. I really did want to tell her one last time that I loved her, and I would have said it if I wasn't thinking about all those bills.

Once the door closes, boy it doesn't matter what you wanted to say. If you didn't say it while they were living, you'll never get the chance to say it after they are gone. I have been very bothered by that. It is strange how I could have been treated the way I was treated and feel badly that I didn't have the chance to say, 'I love you,' to a person that never loved me. I can't explain that because it doesn't make any sense, but that's the way it was.

You may not always get what you deserve, but usually you do get what you resist. Kitty's biggest fear was to die alone and that's exactly what she attracted. She died alone in her soiled twin bed, in the upstairs bedroom of a decaying row house, and my guess would be that the angels didn't even come for her. She left behind a load of personal debt, a dilapidated row house, and a legacy of cruelty and abuse. Ironically, Kitty was buried in the Odd Fellows Cemetery. The Odd Fellows is an ancient organization that promotes personal and social development. Members of the organization dedicate their entire lives to improving and elevating the character of humankind, to making the world a better place to live in, and to promoting good will and harmony.[25] Although she was undeniably odd, it could be argued that Kitty was not worthy of burial in such a sacred place. The only redeeming quality is that although she didn't personally contribute to making the world a better place, she did give birth to two magnificent human beings who would.

21

Second Chances

*"Don't close the book when bad things happen,
just turn the page and begin a new chapter."*
–Unknown

In the 1980s Allen's construction business was thriving and so was his music career. He was on the road regularly with his Canyon River Band and performing and shopping his songs in Nashville every chance he got. Through this, Allen came to know and work with many famous country music artists. Roy Clark, who also resided with his wife in the Baltimore area became good friends with Allen. Not only did they have country music in common, but also shared an affinity for thoroughbred horse racing. When Roy suggested Allen buy a racehorse of his own, he did, but it turned out to be just another of life's tough lessons for him.

Laurel, Maryland is known for its horse racing, and there were a lot of racetracks around where we lived. We kept several thoroughbred racehorses on our farm, and I would frequent the racetrack. I knew Roy Clark from our time together in Nashville and he was from the Washington D.C. area, so we often went to the races together. He and his wife Barbara lived nearby and kept a stable full of racehorses, and of course, I would be interested in the horse that he would be running on the day of the race. Roy was just this happy, delightful guy, and we had a fun time together. A lot of people approached him wanting to shake his hand, and get their pictures taken with him, and he never denied anyone. He talked me into attending a horse claiming race and he picked out a beautiful and spirited horse by the name of Kiera Elena which meant "Bold Lady" in Greek. She was a three-year-old filly, and they wanted three thousand dollars to claim her.

With friend Roy Clark

In a horse claiming race, you put up the money to buy the horse before the race even starts. If this horse wins the race, all winnings go to the current owner, but then the horse becomes yours. If the horse you are claiming before the race drops dead for any reason, then you just bought yourself a dead horse. At this horse claiming race, I did get the filly, Kiera Elena, and I trailered her back to the farm. I entered her in a few races after that, but she consistently finished in fifth or sixth place, never really getting into big money. It wasn't long before she came down with the horse flu, and the vet bills were piling up.

At the time, I had a dishonest horse trainer who was rigging it so that the filly never won a race. I really wanted my good friend and top jockey at the time, Vincent Bracciale Jr. to ride her for me, but my trainer insisted on selecting his own jockeys to ride. It was unbelievably crooked, but they were holding her back on purpose. He made excuses for each lost race, explaining that it was because she needed to wear blinkers, or that she kept swallowing her tongue while running. So, I bought blinkers, and they tied her tongue and still no wins. I did everything my trainer suggested and yet from the time I claimed her, she never won a single race. No money was coming in and I was left paying all her expenses so I concluded that I couldn't afford to keep doing that.

The trainer assured me that he would wipe the financial slate clean if I turned ownership of the horse over to him. I had no choice but to agree to that, but just a week later, I received a call from the Delaware Downs wondering why I never came by for my purse. 'My purse? What purse?' My horse Kiera Elena won a twenty-thousand-dollar purse and I had to tell them that I no longer owned her. The trainer held the horse back every race so it wouldn't win, racked up the bills, and then tricked me into handing her over to him. That was my introduction to horse racing, and it was really a learning experience for me. I can assure you I never did anything like that again.

Allen was growing weary of not spending quality time with his wife because it seemed like when he was home in Maryland, he was working around the clock. Even though they occupied the same residence, Darlene never showed any interest in the things he was working on outside of their home. She never worked side-by-side with him on a project, although she did come outside occasionally to admire the work he finished. When his in-laws moved in on their lives, it took its toll in so many ways. His home was no longer the place where he felt supported and loved. In his mind, he became the outsider and the third wheel to Darlene's relationship with her mother. It seemed like Darlene no longer cared about Allen and he found comfort on the road with his bandmates.

The stage was one place where the spotlight shined directly on Allen, and the applause and attention of adoring fans was just what his banged-up self-esteem needed. Affirmations, recognition, and success fueled Allen and the more he got, the more he wanted, and it was a bit addictive that way. Having a husband who is the lead singer of a traveling band, with beautiful women around him, begging for pictures, wrapping their arms around him and being flirtatious is not an easy road for even the most confident of women.

Darlene understood that it was his music keeping Allen youthful, and it provided its natural medicine to heal his soul. It wasn't that she no longer cared about her husband, wasn't attracted to him, or worried about him leaving her and the kids for another woman, it was simply that she trusted him. Darlene graciously gave her husband the loving freedom and full rein to pursue his dreams without jealousy. By doing so, she honestly believed that she was showing him the greatest love of all. Allen was her soulmate and her one true love so you can only imagine the deep hurt she felt when he broke her trust. Allen began having an affair with the wife of a close hunting buddy. The other woman worked as an assistant to the administrator where AK Construction was doing remodeling work. What started out as a kind hello, a friendly smile, and an innocent hug, turned into eating lunch together, and before long, a full-blown affair ensued. Finding out her husband was seeing someone else on the side, completely crushed Darlene.

I am not sure how Darlene found out, but one day, I came to the apartment to visit the woman I was having an affair with, and before I could knock, the door opened. She tentatively greeted me, 'Hi Allen. We've got company.' I walked through her door to see Darlene sitting in the living room where the two of them had been talking. I immediately knew my unfaithfulness hurt Darlene deeply, and that crushed me to see her this way. In a calm voice, Darlene told me, 'Well, I can see why you would want to be here, with everything so tidy and in its place. Allen, if you want to come home, I will be there.' Going home to her and the kids was exactly what I wanted and needed to do and so I ended the affair that very moment. Cheating on Darlene was the biggest mistake of my life. I took her trust in me for granted and have hated myself for it ever since. I wished with all my heart that I could take back all the pain that I caused her that day.

Darlene welcomed her husband back, but what else could she do? There were bills, a full house to feed, a grooming business to run, young children to raise and unbeknownst to Allen, another baby was on its way. Darlene knew that there was no leaving her marriage, so she began trying to strengthen it once again.

Staircase Lounge inside the Opryland
Hotel in Nashville, Tennessee

In the early 1980s, Allen wasn't home much because of his music, and he was in Nashville to shop his songs to labels and producers. For those three months, he shared an apartment with a fellow entertainer, promoting his music by day and playing the Staircase Lounge at the Opryland Hotel by night. At the time, he was signed again with Sundial Records which was based in Nashville, so it made sense for him to be there full-time. There was never another woman in the picture after his affair, and Darlene was making a deliberate effort to stay in her husband's life. Setting responsibilities at home aside, she made the trip to Nashville several times to support Allen in his music. She stayed with him and attended his shows, and together, they enjoyed the bond they once knew.

Time spent together was a second chance for Allen, and when Darlene revealed that she was pregnant for a fourth and final time, there was no doubt in his mind that God was granting them both another blessing. Even though Allen was forty-three years old at the time and there was a fourteen-year age gap between their first-born and the baby on the way, this child would be the glue they so desperately needed to hold the family together. Not all were thrilled however, and when Allen shared the news that they were expecting a fourth child, Darlene's mother went crazy and attempted to jump out of the moving car. Despite Laura's temper tantrum that day, Darlene scheduled a C-Section and brought Amanda Laura Katherine Sterner into the world on April 15, 1983.

Thankfully, Darlene never stopped loving me. She showed me how to love, and what it means to love and care for someone. She always said to me, 'I wish you loved me as much as I love you.' I did love her in my own way, but I feel as though I deprived her of a "true love."

My past was something I could never revisit, it was gone, it was over, and I survived. I came out on the other end of a terrible battle and that was it, but without Darlene, I don't know what my situation would be today. She honestly saved my life and enabled me to be strong and take risks that she would never have been able to take alone. All because she believed in my ability to find a way to turn any failure into a success. She stood in the wings, confident I was going to pull it off, and I knew if I fell, she'd catch me. I didn't want her to ever have to do that, so I worked extremely hard to make it all happen for us.

From 1979 until 1992 Allen's construction business was going strong. In 1992 a recession hit, and work was nowhere to be found. Then a destructive hurricane hit Dade County, Florida, and the positive aspect in the aftermath of the destruction of homes, was plentiful work for those like Allen who needed it most.

To bring in extra money on the side, I sold tomatoes, firewood, and Silver Queen corn, to individuals operating roadside stands in the area. They came to our farm to pick everything up and paid me sixty cents per dozen. It was a help, but we still struggled to pay our utilities. Luckily, we had a well for water, so we didn't have to pay for that, but it was overall a grim time.

Hurricane Andrew hit hard and there were seven hundred and fifty thousand roofs taken off by the storm. As a roofer myself, I wanted to help people rebuild. The local Spencerville Church wanted me to drive a bus filled with students including my daughter, Becky, to Dade County to help church members in need. By doing so, I was able to see first-hand the total devastation. It was like a war zone with refrigerators stuck in trees, and it was the worst sight you can imagine, because it looked like a bomb went off. On the other hand, I saw opportunities for long-term work which I needed more than ever. After a week, I drove the bus and kids back to Maryland and explained to Darlene that I had to return. This was perfect timing because

I wired funds back home to pay down our mounting bills. Our mortgage was at least three months behind, and we had already received one letter from the bank warning us that our farm would be sold at auction if we missed just one more payment.

Allen spent three months in Florida without a place to stay. He slept in the back of his brand-new Suburban he fondly called "Cody." He went without electricity, restrooms, and the atmosphere was very hectic. Helicopters flew all over the place because looting and crime were at elevated levels and one can only imagine that a brand-new Suburban parked out there drew some attention. Unaware that Allen was sleeping in the back, thieves tried to steal his car. When Allen jumped out and chased them across the parking lot madly swinging his four-foot metal level, they took off running. His overnight parking rotated between three different shopping centers and every morning he brought his cooler to Burger King for supplies. The staff gave him bacon and egg biscuits, free coffee, and generous scoops of ice to chill the daily provisions he filled his cooler with.

My Suburban was a lifeline out there. It was a hotel, restaurant, and my only means of hauling all supplies to the job site. I'd pick up the roofing supplies in my truck each day from Home Depot where they had tractor trailers outside and they would load me up from there. With so much roofing going on in the county, the materials never had the chance to make it inside the store before being sold and it was a madhouse. I found a roofless house nearby that nobody lived in where the water worked, and I took my cold showers in there. It was hot and miserable outside so the cold showers were very refreshing.

More than likely, I would have stayed in Florida and worked much longer than three months, if it weren't for the Cuban Mafia in the area. One evening, I happened to be in a laundromat standing in the back where the washers were located. It was just me and this old man at that time of day. Of course, the matron of the laundromat was there too which turned out to be a lucky break for me. A pregnant woman entered, followed by a man who attacked her – slamming her down on her back. In the commotion, she managed to kick the bubblegum machine over, and colorful gumballs rolled everywhere. Instinctively, I went to her defense, and I never got the chance to help her up to her feet before the man took a swing at me. I put his head through the dryer door as two more men came at me. I hit the second guy extremely hard, and he fell to the ground, sending the third guy running away.

It wasn't over and the mob boss walked right up to my face. He was impeccably dressed and not at all amused with what I did to his guys. He took a black card painted with three red dots out of his pocket and threw it down at my feet, then walked away. Luckily, the matron of the laundromat witnessed everything and called the police. I showed the card to the officer, and he explained that the card meant that the mafia was threatening me. Each red dot represented blood and the mob would make three attempts on my life until they succeeded in killing me. If they missed me after three attempts, then I was free, and they would never try again. There were three blood red dots on that card, but the police warned me that the mob never missed on their first attempt. They strongly advised me to leave town that same night because they couldn't protect me.

I did leave town, but not that night. I finished the project I was working on and came home for Christmas. By that time, there was enough work in Maryland to keep the bills paid, so I never returned to Florida. It was a troubled time, but you know, through the tough times you learn the most. They teach you that you must rise above it, and you can't succumb to it. This is what you must get over, and you work at that and just know in your mind that it isn't going to cause you to fail. Tell yourself, 'I am going to be fine,' and work towards that every day. Sometimes you lay your head down on the pillow at night and you're thinking, 'Oh my gosh, today was really something. Tomorrow has to be a better day!'

Working on a roof in 1983, Allen slipped and fell eighteen feet, landed on his side, and laid there feeling dead. Doctors weren't sure if he would ever walk again and for weeks following the accident he was confined to a wheelchair. Determined to walk again, he lifted himself out of the chair and practiced walking while no one was home. Whenever he fell, he just dragged himself back to the wheelchair and tried again. Over time, he did regain his ability to walk, and it was all because he refused to accept any other outcome.

If you asked Allen which he preferred, a vacation at the beach or in the mountains, he would choose the mountains because he is a mountain man at heart. If his soul needed recharging, you would find him exploring the woods with a trusty compass in hand. Always an avid outdoors person, he especially enjoyed the hunting camps in Northern Maine. He loved the camaraderie and making life-long friends with one man, who would have a profound impact on him.

Janet's husband had a wonderful uncle named Monroe Daniel. I was in my late fifties when I first shook his hand saying, 'I am glad to meet you Mr. Daniel.' He told me to call him "UNK," so from that point forward he was UNK to me and became an incredibly special person in my life. He was the managing supervisor of the Pennsylvania Power and Light Company. His job was to transfer power to different states as they needed and purchased it from his company. He worked hard, but every vacation was spent hunting and fishing with me. UNK and his wife, Marge came to the picnics at our Johnnycake Road farm, and we always shared good times. I'd say to him, 'UNK, I am planning a fishing trip,' and he would ask, 'When do we leave?' I hunted with him in Maine, Canada, and Pennsylvania, and fished with him in South Carolina. We specifically loved the Red River Camps in Maine and UNK was just this avid hunter and fisherman.

He was the kind of man who believed he was helping the herd by thinning them out, making the ones that remained, stronger, and the breeding lines better. He could give you a whole list of reasons why you should hunt and take a deer every year. There were many times I hunted with him, but never standing side-by-side. We carefully placed each other in different sections of the woods far enough away to not shoot towards each other. I spotted some of the most beautiful bucks in those woods. I'd put my crosshairs on a deer and go over its entire body with the scope and think, 'What a magnificent animal!' I put the crosshairs right on its face and it would look around like it was saying something to me, 'Bang! I got you!' The hardest part of it all was telling UNK that I didn't see anything because he would have been extremely disappointed to know that I let a buck like that go.

UNK loved that hunting camp and used to tell me all the time that he would die there, and he did. He died right there in my cabin. It was close to five o'clock in the morning and I heard him call out to me that he was in trouble. I rushed into his bedroom, and he was having difficulty breathing. UNK was on oxygen, and when I checked his bottles, they were about empty. I grabbed one of his oxygen bottles and drove for an hour and a half just to get out of the woods and to a hospital. I knew nothing about oxygen, but I found out you needed a prescription to refill it. I explained that it was an emergency and that there was a man in the hunt camp desperately in need of it, yet they still wouldn't fill it. They told me to contact his primary care physician and I had no idea who that was. They finally contacted the hospital in Potter County, Pennsylvania and found his doctor to fill out a prescription.

Allen far left and UNK far right at the cabin where UNK died

Four hours later, I returned to the camp, and personnel stopped me at the gate. They knew who I was and told me that my dearest friend, UNK, had already passed away. The coroner arrived in a big winter storm that was hitting at the same time, and they couldn't get the ambulance back there to retrieve the body. We loaded UNK into the back of my Suburban and took him out to where the ambulance was waiting. There were about thirty-five hunters in the camp, and you could see them across the mountainside because they were all dressed in bright orange snow suits. They all took their hats off and placed them over their hearts as we passed. UNK hunted there for thirty-five years, and everyone thought the world of him. The camp was a

*beautiful place to live and die with authentic log cabins built
many years ago. It was 1996 when I lost UNK and to this day,
I've never gone back into the woods hunting. In fact, all my
hunting guns haven't been fired since that trip either. He was
an incredible man and I miss him so much.*

Allen's greatest exhilaration came from ultimate wilderness
adventures. The kind that forces you to wring out every drop of
survival skill, just to make it out alive.

*I did "fly-ins" to Third Saint John above Greenville, Maine.
I absolutely fell in love with it there with Moosehead Lake and
the area's abundant wildlife. My favorite part was eating in one
of their cozy cafes watching a moose just strolling down the
middle of the street. I'd have Folsom Air Service fly me into the
wilderness and drop me off for a week. I've ventured out there
alone, but there were times when friends joined me as well. I
traveled there with my best friend and lead carpenter, Donny,
and my favorite horseracing jockey Vincent Bracciale Jr. whom
we fondly called, "Jimbo." We'd set up our tents and pulled
out dried food to mix with water and cook over a campfire. I
explored the area and discovered bear dens which I entered
smelling for any recent activity. The scent of a bear is unmistakable
because they stink from not taking regular baths.*

*I realized when that plane was out of sight, it wouldn't return
for a week. If I suffered appendicitis or a heart attack, I was
going to die. I accepted that and there was no false pretense
about it. I understood that I had to be careful while rock climbing,
and mindful of vines covering holes in the ground where I could
break something and lay there. There was no radio contact
whatsoever, so I had no way of reaching anybody. Hundreds of
miles from civilization and I felt the pure adrenaline within me.*

I could catch rainbow trout all day long. The lakes were virgin, brimming with fish and I could use the slightest little silver hook in the water, and they latched on every time. I did this every year and one time, I found a small trapper's cabin with its roof leaking. There were no supplies or anything, but it looked like someone had been there. I found things like that while exploring and I always kept a compass with me. In the woods you must be careful not to get lost. I'd love to move to Maine, live in a cabin, and have a black bear cub named Cody to raise as my friend. It's a dream of mine, but as long as I am alive, it's not too late for me.

Trapper cabins, bear caves, and wildlife havens weren't the only things Allen unearthed in his adventure-filled adulthood. The greatest discovery of all, was finding a way to break the cycle of abuse set in motion by his maternal grandmother. Abuse is not infinite – it can be ended. The flow can be reversed and sent in an entirely new direction with a swift current of unconditional love. And that's exactly what Allen managed to do when it came to raising his own family.

22

Curbing the Flow

"Didn't it break your heart when you watched my smile fading?
Did it ever cross your mind, that one day the tables would be turned?
They told me the best revenge, would be a life well-lived. And the
strongest one that holds, would be the hardest one to earn."
–Brandi Carlile

A life well lived is the best revenge, and Allen took it much farther than that by breaking the cycle of abuse within his own family. He created the type of home life for his children that he desperately yearned for himself. When you are used to having so little, how are you capable of creating a life of plenty for others? Plenty of love, laughter, freedom, and fond memories. Most often, our best lessons in life come from what not to do, and to rise above our past we simply need to do the exact opposite of what was done to us. Allen was intelligent enough to learn from his past and became the type of family-oriented person that his father never was. This was Allen's secret to successfully breaking the cycle of violence. It's extremely difficult to imagine that it could be that simple, but Allen made parenting look easy, which is truly remarkable considering his background. Everyone wants to know how to create a life void of abuse when all you've ever known is a life full of abuse. It's like asking a rose to grow and thrive out of barren soil, while praying for yesterday's rain.[26]

My kids have no idea what it's like living as I did. Thank God!
That's why I always protected them. I could never hit my children
because my mom wasn't able to stop herself until she was in pain

and hurting her own fist. I could never take a chance on spanking or hitting my children, because I was afraid that I couldn't stop either. No, I never touched my children. I never slapped them, not even once, and of course, I would never hit or hurt my wife. As a child, I was brutalized and have always been against anybody that would say they hit and beat their wives and children because they were hit and beat themselves. My comeback to that is if you love your children or wife, how can you inflict pain on them? How can you do that and still claim to love them? I guess in a lot of ways, I didn't think that my mom ever loved me. She couldn't have done the unspeakable things that she did to me and still have loved me.

Left to right: Rebecca, Amanda, Travis and Janelle

Darlene always thought that she was the only disciplinarian in the family, and she was. I'd say, 'Yes. Yes, you are the only disciplinarian. So, do what you must, but don't ask me to do it.

I'll talk to my children, but that's it.' I never yelled at my children either – I could just give them a certain look and they knew I meant business. I always believed the worst chewing out you could get is one where somebody uses an incredibly low voice, but every word is penetrating. To scream something in somebody's face, I mean, that just blows by them. That soft, but serious tone of voice, is the worst that you can get. I have been yelled at so much as a child, I developed a hardened sense to it. You just close your ears and almost don't remember what was said because it was so loud. Darlene wasn't one for giving spankings or anything like that. If the kids acted up, all she had to do was make believe she was going to get that small paddle and boy, they straightened right up. All my children were good children growing up and now they have wonderful kids of their own and they call me "Poppy," and Darlene was "Nana." So, we were Poppy and Nana to all of them and they are all terrific. My six grandchildren mean the world to me, and I am so proud of them all. To Mitchell, Lilly, Olivia, Caleb, Anabelle, and Violet – 'Poppy dearly loves you all.'

For years, Allen and Darlene hosted gatherings on their beautiful farm. Bringing the family together became a tradition they started when they were still in their Cape Cod home. Families traveled from Pennsylvania and there were memorable fourth of July picnics. Crowds came to the farm and Allen entertained with his Canyon River Band. Kids would play, swim, and pet the farm animals. Christmas on the farm was a special time as well. Darlene loved that time of year most of all, and the Christmas Eve gatherings were sometimes larger than the picnics during the summer. There were homemade baked cookies and gifts for everyone. The love that emanated from that farm drew people to it like moths to a brilliant bulb burning in the night. The atmosphere was welcoming, fun-loving, and generous, and it created some of the fondest memories. Darlene and Allen had upbringings that were as different as day and night. Darlene's positive childhood experiences helped to create an atmosphere in her own home that oozed love. Having parents like Darlene and Allen was a blessing, and the children they raised are all very aware of that fact.

Janelle reminisces:

For me, my dad was my ride or die. I was privileged to grow up on a farm. I ran in the fields until I was breathless. I hiked in the woods until I could say that I touched every tree. I rode my horse until I felt like I myself could fly. I memorized each distinctive smell of hay, horse manure, sweet feed, and leather, until they saturated the barnwood. The freedom of the farm's vast openness felt liberating and exciting. What a tremendous high of limitless possibilities. My family was the happiest while living there because the house was constantly filled with life. We had many family reunions, pool parties, picnics and visitors because my family loved to entertain. We always liked a good get together, or the impromptu disco dance party around our dining room table to ABBA's song, 'Dancing Queen.' My parents made us have fun and I never once, throughout my entire childhood, felt unloved. Even when Dad got mad at me for staying out late, the next day we hugged and laughed. Our family smiles a lot and sometimes, it might seem obnoxious, but it really is a natural state. It's an honest happiness and we all got along so well.

I have always had a heightened level of sensitivity. I remember when I was around ten years old, suddenly grabbing my dad and hugging him crying, 'I don't ever want you to die!' He gently pulled me back and said, 'I will always find my way back to you.' 'How?' To answer me, he showed me all the signs of nature like a bird with a beautiful song, a lady bug that gently lands on your arm, the trees blowing, a bee working so hard to nurture the earth with its pollen. He taught me the earth's language and how I would know that he would always find his way back to me. My dad is the one that taught me everything I know about nature. He would go into the woods feeling down and worn out and emerge with this radiant glow. Dad knew how to inspire my relationship with Jesus outside of the church by taking me on a hike in the Fall and teaching me that I could hear God in the leaves crunching beneath our feet. Or feel God's touch on my back as I nudged my horse into a full gallop; or learn patience by having me wait for a fish to jump on my line; or find beauty in the simplicity of walking through a field of flowers, realizing that God is everywhere, if your heart is open.

Dad never said a mean word to me and had the patience of Job, from the Bible. I pushed him to his limits so many times and my biggest rebellion was staying out late on a date or coming in late from a party. Although he was upset about it, he never once pulled back to throw a punch, he would just turn and walk away. Plus, he went out of his way to make sure that he married someone that was the most incredible mother; she was very loving to us and everything his mother wasn't for him. Mom tried to make it work with my dad by balancing everything at home so he could be in Nashville to keep his music going. I know that was one of the things she never wanted him to give up, and before she died, she made me promise that I would keep my dad singing because without music, he wouldn't be here. Their relationship took a lot of love, and my mother must have been more evolved than most because she took on a relationship that not just anyone would have been able to manage. I don't think I would have been able to handle such an independent man as my father. Their love for each other was unconditional, which means to me continuing to love someone despite all the messed-up stuff inside.

Dad tends to forget his kindness, but he's an excellent listener and listens to every word with a look of sincerity. He will always *try to make me laugh when I am crying and give me a hug. I went to my dad one time, and I told him that I thought I was going to have sex and just wanted him to know. I told him that before I was going to do this, I thought it would be best if I got on the pill. He said, 'Oh, really? You've thought this out, huh? Do you feel completely comfortable with this guy?' 'Yes, I love him,' I told my dad. I was crying and he hugged me and was trying to get me to laugh. 'Well, I guess you gotta do what you gotta do.' This was our conversation and then he hugged me and said, 'You will always be my little girl.'*

Do you remember when you felt goosebumps for the first time? I do! I was eight years old, sitting on top of my dad's shoulders, watching Elvis Presely, live in concert. He was singing 'How Great Thou Art.' It was my first concert and I had never experienced the passion or high one can get from one song until that day. It is a precious memory, and it was the first time I was taught how to connect with God, through song. Who would have ever thought that I'd find God at an Elvis Presely concert on the shoulders of my father. I never felt that way before, even inside of a church.

Elvis concert tickets

For Travis, having a good father was especially important and he did everything he could to please his father and gain his approval. He shadowed Allen around the farm and worked with him every chance he got.

Growing up, my dad never had to punish me, and I never got a slap of any kind. All he had to do was give me this look and I knew I'd better shape up. I feared my dad, not that he did anything towards me, but because I always wanted to please him. For some reason, I just wanted to make him happy. In return for pleasing him, I would get joy and happiness. Once he gave me a smile or a 'Good job, Buddy!' I was happy. He always told me I was his right-hand man growing up and that made my day.

He carried a tremendous amount of influence in my life regarding respecting others, especially my elders, and taught me to never talk back. My dad was always in good standing with everybody. He paid his debts on time, he worked hard, and he was a man of his word. If he said it, you could believe it. He would just make things happen.

He spoiled me to no end, and I know there were things he couldn't afford, but he wanted to see that smile on my face, I guess. I don't know if it was because I helped him so much, but he never had to buy me anything. I got a horse, I had my own dog, a bicycle, a dirt bike, go-kart, and we had a swimming pool. He even bought an old VW Bug to teach us how to drive on the farm. Janelle would get that car stuck and dad would have to come and pull her out with the tractor, but we had a lot of fun. I was very sheltered and all I knew was my family. My grandmother paid for me to go to a private church school, and my parents would drive me a good twenty-five minutes one way, every day to get me there. When I turned sixteen, my dad got me my first car which was a 1968 Carmen Ghia.

I have special memories with my dad. We took fishing trips every May down to Santee Cooper in South Carolina. We caught mammoth sized Rock Fish and Blue Catfish, nonstop. When I received my driver's license I got away from things, but he has been an incredible support system for me my whole life. Everyone has always been amazed at how he didn't have a father to teach him, and he didn't have to physically discipline his kids after all the beatings he took from his mother. He never abused any one of us mentally, physically, or spiritually. My dad was more work oriented. 'You got to work, Travis. You gotta work.' He took care of us all and he made things get done when they needed to be done.

If he saw me slacking, he just pulled me aside and had a talk with me. Let me give you an example. I wanted to quit high school in the tenth grade, and he put the fear of God in me and said, 'Travis, you will graduate, and that's final!' It took me five years to get out of high school, but I got my diploma. If it hadn't been for my dad, I would've quit. My dad believes in second chances, and he never gives up on me. What doesn't kill you, makes you a stronger type of man, and his coping mechanism is that he keeps himself busy. I never saw my dad sitting in a chair reading a book or watching TV during the day. He was always into something, and it was all good things to benefit the property, his family, himself, or somebody else. He rarely bought himself things but enjoyed buying other people things.

In the meeting rooms of Alcoholics Anonymous, it seems if people come from trouble, they are trouble too. I've heard others share their stories, insisting that their parents were rotten, and they swore they wouldn't be like them, but somehow, they turned out to be just like them. So, it is rare that my dad didn't turn out to be just like his parents and broke that cycle of abuse.

For Allen and Darlene, Travis was the most difficult of their four children to raise. They were blessed with a beautiful son and as far as they knew at that time, he was a healthy and happy little boy. At least physically he was healthy, but mentally he wasn't developing as expected. Travis's first-grade teacher called home requesting a meeting to discuss the fact that Travis found it difficult to stay focused and as a result, was falling behind in class. She strongly suggested further testing, and that's exactly what Allen and Darlene did.

First grade Travis Sterner

My son was my little shadow on the farm, wanting to follow me all over the place. As a family we had a fun time, taking vacations together, and everything was fine until Travis entered the first grade. We took him to the Kennedy Institute in Baltimore for several weeks of testing. The doctors determined that at birth, a part of Travis's brain didn't fully develop. However, they were optimistic that it would catch up as he grew, providing there was no drug or alcohol use during his adolescent years. Unfortunately, that is what happened unbeknownst to us. Wanting to fit in with his peers, my son engaged in drinking and drugs as a teenager. This behavior caused a deficit in

*normal cognitive and behavioral functioning, and it seemed
impossible to get him to graduate high school. I was determined
that he would at least earn his diploma and it took him five
years to do so. We went around and round with each other every
morning because he didn't want to go to school. I would take
him to school and speak with his teachers to see what we could
do at home to support him and help him study for his tests so
he could pass.*

When a recession hit in 1992, work was hard to find, and Allen
was forced to travel to Florida. This move meant that Travis, now
twenty-one, would have to change jobs as well. After graduation he
lived at home and went to work for his dad in construction, relying
solely on this for income. Knowing this was the situation, Allen had
to find a different job for Travis before he could feel good about
leaving the state. A good friend of Allen's was high up in the FedEx
Company and Allen reached out to him for the favor. Travis was hired
as a courier for FedEx and spent the next twelve years with the
company. In fact, he was considered their top courier; always arriving
early, working overtime, delivering the company's largest route,
and overall doing an exemplary job. Travis loved his career, but
unfortunately, he loved his escapes from reality far more. Alcohol
along with a strong cocaine addiction cost Travis his beloved career
and sent him spiraling down for the rest of his life.

*We never suspected cocaine because he lived at home and
seemed fine, plus he reassured me he wasn't doing any of that.
The company conducted a random urine test on him, and it
showed that he had cocaine in his system. Management sent him
a message to take the keys out of the truck and wait for another
employee to retrieve his packages and drive him back to head-
quarters, where he was immediately fired. Losing his career dealt*

him a terrible blow and he started drinking heavily. Travis is an alcoholic and a drug addict. To date, I have admitted him in at least twenty-five rehabilitation centers, personally costing me half a million dollars. I admitted him with a hefty deposit, and he simply walked out. I rented a fully furnished apartment for him, bailed him out of jail, arranged for meaningful employment and counseling, picked up hotel bills, airline tickets, and absolutely anything I could do to get him back on his feet. I even secured psychiatric help for him, but within three days, they released him back to the streets telling me nothing was wrong with him.

The system is failing us all. In one month, just this past year, Travis was taken by ambulance and detoxed in the emergency room twenty-three times. There are hospitals now that refuse to admit him because he won't commit to getting the help that he needs and falls right back into the same habits. Doctors tell him his internal organs can't stand much more and it's a miracle he is still alive. It's a father's heartache knowing that my son is homeless, drunk, and vulnerable. He's been attacked, beaten up, and robbed of everything-wallet, change, and phone. He has ended up in trap houses where illicit drugs are sold. People like Travis are trapped into selling drugs and taking drugs and these houses are extremely hard to escape from.[27] He is into every bad thing you can imagine and now, he is sitting in jail. At least I know where he is. I know that he is safe, and I also know now that I've done all I could to save him. No amount of external love or money can save him now – the key is self-love and only Travis can change his ways. No one can know what his future will bring, but as his father, I pray every day that it will be a good one.

When Travis consumed alcohol, it made him mean and on more than one occasion he confronted his dad, egging him on to fight back. Allen stood his ground and there was nothing Travis could do or say to make his dad angry enough to strike back and allow the cycle of abuse in his family to keep turning.

When he's drunk, Travis gets mean and calls me everything under the sun. He would swing his fist at me, landing punches in the chest-leaving terrible black and blue marks. One day after Darlene had passed away, Travis was screaming and throwing punches at me on the front porch of our farm. I was recovering from double hernia surgery, and he was screaming at me to stand up and fight him. I couldn't stand up, but even if I could, I would never have retaliated or hurt my son in any way. I was deflecting his blows the best I could, but his rage was escalating. Out of nowhere a pure white dove landed at the base of the stairs and looked up at us. I never in my life had seen a white dove in the wild and it startled us both. That dove flew around the farmhouse several times and landed again in the same place looking up at us. In our hearts we both felt like that was the spirit of Darlene coming to bring peace that day. It worked! The situation was immediately diffused. That same dove returned the following day and I know in my heart that it was Darlene just making sure that everything was still okay.

Thirty-eight years of terrible torment for a man that has already endured more than his share of hardships. The worry and stress are endless and unfortunately, there is no amount of money that can save Travis now. The odds are stacked against him. Recovery rates are less than thirty-six percent for people with a severe or lifetime alcohol dependence.[28] Nevertheless, Allen has never given up hope that there will come a day that Travis will find the internal strength and self-love to fight this terrible disease that holds him prisoner.

Everybody told meto show tough love, and that's what I am doing now by not helping him financially. The only help I now extend is to talk with him every day and offer support and inspiration to give him hope. Tough love, believe me, takes a lot of strength, and will power. It consumes my life to the point where I can't get him out of my mind, and I am waiting for someone to call me and tell me that my son is dead. I don't know who is going through the most pain, him, or me? I wanted the best for my son, and I've backed down to the point where I just want him to live. I always envision being able to visit him and his wife and my grandchildren and we could go fishing again. That's a dream I can't believe will ever come true, but it was a beautiful dream while it lasted.

Becky came along at a time when her dad was away from home more often than not. She was very much a mommy's girl and didn't always feel like she knew her dad as well as her siblings did. Knowing that Becky needed to spend more time with him, Allen made every effort to make up for lost time when he was home. The farm was the only home that Becky knew growing up, and it was a place she never wanted to leave because it was her safe haven.

I was born and raised in the same house until I was in my late twenties. My parents were both very loving, although when I was little, my dad worked a lot, and I didn't see him much. I remember being home and it being my safe place, and the only place I ever wanted to be. I didn't leave home until I was twenty-seven years old because I felt the most love there. Discipline was very lenient, and if you didn't do what you were supposed to do, the consequence was a stern talking to. My dad never physically disciplined, but all he had to do was give you a look or talk in a way that you were never going to want to do that again.

It was pure freedom-going outside whenever I wanted, exploring the woods, and we had animals all the time to play with. Mom and Dad just wanted to make us feel special and never wanted us to fear them or be afraid to come and talk; it was an interesting dynamic. They wanted us to be open, honest, and tried keeping the heavier issues much lighter, happier, and without conflict. Dad is a people pleaser and will agree with everything just to avoid conflict with anyone. I do believe his music career was a huge coping skill which helped a lot and allowed him to be somebody he couldn't be at home. He needed recognition and he couldn't get that at home. As kids, we were like, 'Great, go sing Dad!' Spending more time at home might have been difficult for him because at home, he wasn't the center of attention.

Dad wanted us to know how well we were taken care of, and we were always provided for. What I admire most about him is that he is the most generous person I've ever known. Whatever he has, it's yours. He has helped me countless times in my life, especially after my divorce. He's very giving of himself and never asks for anything in return, and I don't deserve everything that he has given to me. His giving spirit humbles me, and I am very moved by his kindness in that regard. Giving us children all that we needed is what really drove him to succeed in life.

When I was young and knew nothing about his upbringing, I saw Dad as this noticeably confident and self-assured person, which was nothing like me. I was more like my mom, and she had a considerable influence on me, especially her kindness. When you were feeling bad about yourself, and thinking life is hard, Mom believed that you should focus on helping others. You will feel much better if you help other people and I tried to do just that.

With Dad, it was just work hard and don't stop until the job is done right, so you won't have to go back and do it again. He is very much a perfectionist, and nothing can be glossed over. I didn't feel like he knew me very well. I was closer to my mom at the time, but he realized I needed time with him, too. We went to the movies, and it was always fun. He laughed and joked and kept things light-hearted. During my elaborate wedding where he paid for everything, he looked me right in the eye and said, 'I don't care about any of this. If this isn't what you want, we're gonna walk back inside.' I know he would have done that for me, no matter how much he had spent.

Amanda was the baby of the family and very much a daddy's girl. At the time she was born, his business was good, things between he and Darlene were getting better, and Allen was home more often. Plus, Allen was older then and entering more of a nurturing stage in his life. The father/daughter memories they created together are strong in Amanda's mind.

You were my very first love, and the man of my dreams. When you came from work, 'Daddy's home!' I would scream. I wanted to be your shadow, follow you all over the farm. Errands to the bank were fun with you, even chores in the garden or barn. I loved our dates at McDonald's. We had our special songs. The uncontrollable giggles in the car always made it hard to sing along. The tickles in the big brown chair. I would always squeal with glee. I tried to get away, you tried to catch me and Daddy, 'I am gonna pee!' Our weddings in the living room, you would walk on your knees to be my height. I loved to have heart-to-heart talks with you and sleep, holding your arm all night. Our fishing trips at Diamond Ridge, putting up the Christmas tree, wherever you were was where I wanted to be. The list of memories goes on and on, these are only a few. But the feeling of joy and love was overwhelming whenever I was with you.

Cherished moments I hold in my heart, they mean the world to me. I'll be Daddy's little girl for all my days. I love you more than you love me. – Me Me.

Allen said that as a baby, Amanda would go around the house saying, "Me, me, me, me!" Those were her first words, so he always called her "Me Me."

I never got into trouble. I could do no wrong and I was very spoiled, I'm not going to lie. I was the spoiled baby, but I was well-behaved too, so I didn't push it. At least I don't think I did. I was very much Daddy's girl. I grew up on that farm and I always lived there. A magical place to grow up and it was traumatic when my dad sold it. He didn't let the pain of losing my mother ease up a bit before making the decision to sell it. At the same time, selling the farm helped to gain some amount of closure. Unlike his own upbringing, my dad never hit, spanked, or abused us. Mom was more of a disciplinarian, but I use that term very lightly because I feel like they both had the motto of, "pick your battles." Even sometimes I would say, 'Well, you gotta pick one!' If anything, my dad's fault was that he didn't set any boundaries, which could not be good for a kid too. I do feel like I expect a lot out of men because my dad set the example, although an unrealistic one.

My favorite thing to do as a kid was spend time together. He took me fishing, and I was lucky because at the point in his life when I came around, he had more time to spend with me than he did with my siblings. I was absolutely his last kid too and even then; he didn't expect me to come around. I only sense gratefulness and gratitude that I was born, and I would like to believe my birth healed something between my parents in some respects. I had this thing where I tried to scare my dad when he walked in the door from work and we had our dates to McDonalds, and fishing trips to Diamond Ridge. We had some good times, and we had a lot of games we played like, I try to get away, and you try to catch me. I'd sit on his lap and try to run off it. He grabbed me and if he got a hold of me, I got tickled. Simple games that I begged him to play, and I am sure that he was so darn tired, yet it was rare that he wouldn't play with me.

When everything was up against Dad, giving up was never an option. He believed there must be a way, and we are going to figure it out. He has never succumbed to defeat in any capacity. A major source of fuel for him, and what fills his cup, is being around people. Being around people who love him and adore him. He wants to hear how great he is, and he is great, so it makes him feel good. Especially coming from where he did, not hearing any of that. I think it has made him seek out the music industry where he gets love from a vast number of fans.

I admire the strength of his mind; he is a very strong-minded person. He has never been a victim and he never let people have power over him. If he's been wronged, he doesn't dwell on it. He's never let anyone have the power over him to make him feel resentful, angry, or bitter. He's always realized that his mind is his own and he can choose to love instead of hate. If my parents were in financial trouble, his motto was, 'I'll make more money.' He's just a resilient man.

The main reason I brought friends to the house is because it was a fun place to be. I remember several friends commenting on the fact that my house just felt good, like there was good energy in it. They felt loved in that house. My parents both wanted my friends around and just thought it was a cool thing that they wanted to be there too.

Even to this day, Amanda, now grown and married with two children of her own, still comes home to Allen's house in Murfreesboro, Tennessee. For the last two years, she has brought her closest girlfriends with her, and they have become fondly known as, "Allen's Angels." Lauren Huttner, Stephanie Fitzpatrick, Molly Higgins, Tina Harlan, Tanya Remsberg, and Amanda are Allen's Angels, and he loves the tradition they have started.

Allen's Angels formed when Mandy called me up one day and told me that she was going to be bringing five of her girlfriends to Nashville to stay with me. She told them, 'Let's go down to Tennessee, and party with my dad!' I can imagine them all thinking, 'Okay, we're going to Tennessee, and we are going to party with your eighty-one-year-old father? Will the nursing home allow that?' The girls had no reservations, and they just looked forward to getting away from their children and husbands on a girls' trip. Mandy introduced me to everyone and while standing in my kitchen I looked at everyone and said, 'I have one rule, and only one rule, while you are here. I want you to pretend that this is your house, and I want you to be able to go to the refrigerator without asking and get anything that you want from there. Help yourselves to anything in the pantry and one last thing, we must have a shot of Fireball, right now!' They said, 'Alright, okay, this is cool. We're going to have fun now.' So that's how I kicked it off, and we all had fun together.

We cooked out on my deck, shopped for cowboy boots in downtown Nashville, and bought shirts from Rippy's, and then we all danced on my back deck and took pictures. Then we went to Tootsie's where on every level, they had a live band playing. We went up to the fourth floor and I bought a round of Fireball shots for everyone, and we had so much fun. We visited Gaylord's Opryland Hotel and had a beautiful dinner together and walked through all the greenery under the atrium. We finished at the Nashville Palace across the street where another great band was playing. I had six girls altogether with me and they were all dancing with guys and doing the two-step. I was standing back with two of the girls and we were watching the others dance. This guy approached them and asked them to dance, so one of the girls danced with him and then came back to me. The man kept looking at me as I was standing there looking over my girls. He finally asked me, 'Are these two girls with you?' I said, 'Yes, they are, and you see the other four girls out there? They are with me too.' He said, 'Oh my heart! Oh, my heart!' He didn't know what I had going for me, but he could hardly believe that all these beauties were there with me.

Allen's Angels – Left to right: Lauren, Stephanie, Tanya, Allen, Mandy, Tina and Molly

Allen's Angels came back to visit me again this year, just before Thanksgiving and helped me put up a Christmas tree and decorate for the holidays. We went downtown again and back to the Nashville Palace, out to Arrington Vineyards, and enjoyed a fireside dinner at the Sportsman's Grill in Cool Springs. Of course, we had our traditional shots of Fireball too.

Allen's Angels have become a fun tradition and I look forward to seeing them here again soon.

Darlene spent most of her adult life doting on her parents and putting them first before her needs or the needs of the marriage and at times, this created frustration and division. When Laura and Fred were both deceased, Darlene allowed herself to turn her full attention and time back to Allen and it rekindled their closeness.

Sometimes, Darlene told me, while her mother was still alive, that she was disgusted with having to take her mother places, and how she was dominating her time. Her mother never drove, but when she wanted to do something or go somewhere, she always insisted that Darlene take her. She'd always do it and it was as if her mother had a spell over her. After her mother passed away, Darlene clung to me, and it seemed like when we were first married. We spent time, just the two of us, and I was loving it. She joined me for lunch on construction sites, and it seemed like, for the first time in years, she was willing to be with me. We ate out more and I took her to my shows in Nashville, Texas, and many other locations. She started to go with me to a few of my concerts and sit quietly in the audience because she didn't want the attention directed towards her. Before I took the stage, she made me promise that I wouldn't announce her presence. My wife never wanted any light shone on her, but I was proud to have her there with me.

Allen was beginning to look less and less like his father and more like his mother and he was aging beyond his years. A picture was taken of Darlene sitting next to him on the front steps of their farmhouse, and he thought he looked incredibly old. In the music business, there is enormous pressure to constantly look your best and for Allen, it was all about his fans. So, out of vanity, he drastically changed his image in the middle of his marriage without first asking Darlene what she thought. He spent thirty thousand dollars and underwent a massive nine-hour surgery to remove his entire face. It was as if he wanted to erase the person looking back at him in the mirror and create and entirely different identity.

There were sixty stitches in each eyelid, grotesque swelling, and the pain was excruciating. Darlene was so upset about it that she refused to stay in the same bedroom or even look at Allen while he was healing. A registered nurse sat bedside with him to make sure he didn't bleed to death during his first few days, but the entire healing process took months. The total transformation of his face was so substantial that it even changed his facial hair shaving patterns. With his youthful new look came increased confidence on stage, but also a sense of guilt. Now he looked so much younger than Darlene and they were supposed to grow old together, but instead, he skipped it and left her behind. Allen offered to pay for a procedure for her as well, but she adamantly refused. He felt so guilty afterwards that if there was a way that he could have undone every bit of it, he would have. Looking much younger now than his wife inevitably created more marital problems, and it put a definite end to Darlene's presence in the audience.

Driver's License Comparison
(Issued June 13, 2002)   (Issued June 8, 2012)

One concert I will never be able to forget was in Kyle, Texas. Darlene came along on tour with me and after the show that evening a fan approached her and made the comment that she must be enormously proud of her son. It hurt her deeply and she wanted to go home that night and not continue touring with me. It was a huge fiasco because I had to drive her all the way back to Nashville to catch a plane and get back to Texas before our next show. After that moment, she never attended another show with me because she never wanted to hear anything like that again.

23

Laura Darlene Sterner
January 3, 1943 to March 12, 2017

*"Above all, love each other deeply. Because love covers over
a multitude of sins."*
–1 Peter 4:8

Weatherwise, this was the most beautiful day we have had all year and it is Good Friday, so I chose to spend the day writing about an incredibly special woman in Allen's life. A special angel that God put on this earth to bring love and light to everyone she met. Darlene was an only child to Laura and Fred Williams, and she was their absolute pride and joy. Her childhood was filled with love, and the memories she had of growing up were the total opposite of Allen's. Darlene's love for Allen created the balance needed in his life and she helped him to overcome some of life's most challenging moments. Darlene herself was full of life, and kindness exuded from her; people couldn't help but be instantly drawn to her. She was beautiful in a very natural way, wearing little to no makeup and simple jewelry such as a modest watch, wedding ring, or an occasional pin. She had the most beautiful smile that always reached her eyes and made them twinkle and she possessed a fun and adventurous spirit.

Darlene told everyone that Allen swept her off her feet and became her one true love and she swore that she'd go anywhere with him in life. She didn't have one doubt in her mind that she was doing the right thing by marrying him, and together, they weathered some of the roughest storms any marriage could face. Darlene's unconditional love showed Allen the way to break the cycle of abuse from childhood, and the two of them created a home filled with love, laughter, games, music, social gatherings, and happiness for their four children and six grandchildren.

Darlene was extremely intelligent and nothing short of a wonder woman running their own pet grooming business while managing a household and raising four children. Darlene loved to be around people and always wanted her house to be full of life. She welcomed everyone with open arms to celebrate holidays for which she loved to spend hours cooking and baking. Her favorite holiday of all was Christmas. She adored baking Christmas cookies, and every gift she gave was so well thought out and her generosity abounded. The family lovingly called her their "Barbara Walters," because she wanted to find out as much about a person as possible. She believed that people liked to talk about themselves, and she encouraged that by asking them lots of questions. Her happiest place was on the Johnnycake Road farm, sitting in her favorite rocking chair surrounded by Allen and her children.

Darlene prided herself on being a faithful servant of God and although she respected all religions, she chose to be a life-long member of the Seventh Day Adventist Church. She could quote verses of the Bible on request and believed with all her heart that heaven would have other people there besides just the followers of her church. She thought God would welcome the people who would be the happiest and find the most contentment being there with Him in heaven. She believed that it was a sin against God himself to be depressed in life and that complaining solved nothing, while gratitude went a long way. She wasn't just a Christian in a meaningless titled sort of way, she lived the Christian way of life to the best of her ability, every single day. She encouraged others to do as she did and helped others with some act of kindness no matter how insignificant it may have seemed.

Darlene was loved and cherished in life and now in death, and to me, that is the highest honor anyone can achieve. The connection that these two special people shared between them is the Holy Grail of relationships. Everyone strives for that perfect balance of love and friendship that lasts beyond a lifetime. I know with all my heart that when Allen is called from this earth, Harvey will guide him to the keeper of the keys to the Kingdom of Heaven, and Darlene will be the first angel there to welcome him home. I know he will be happy, and for the first time in a long, long time, Allen's soul will be at peace.

Christmas Cuddle

Allen never expected his wife to pass before him, and that's why he started getting things together for her at the farm. He knew if he died, it would all be too much for her to deal with, so he sold trailers, equipment, tractors, and countless other things. I am sure that Allen would rather die than face the world of pain he experienced when Darlene became sick and passed away.

In 2013, Darlene fell ill. She woke up one morning blind in one eye. The doctors determined that she suffered a stroke in that eye causing the blindness. The clot blocked the blood flow going to the retina and took away her eyesight. Then she came down with Parkinson's and Osteoporosis. One day while working in the closet, she broke three vertebrae in her back simply by taking too many heavy clothes off their hangers at once. She was bent over terribly which caused lung issues preventing her from taking a deep breath.

She spent three months in a nursing home, and I visited her every single day. She was on a respirator and unable to eat because the disease affected the little flap which prevents food from going down into your lungs. Ventilators, feeding tubes, and watching her endure so much was such an awful time for the both of us. I planned to take her back home to care for her there, but she died just before I could make that happen. It was March 12, 2017. I spent time with her earlier that day and left the nursing home when she drifted off to sleep. As soon as I got back to our farm, the hospital called me and said that she had passed away.

Laura Darlene Sterner

After Darlene passed, I tried to stay on the farm, but I just couldn't do it. People may find it strange, but when you're married for as long as we were, you have a sense about each other that most people never enjoy. We could be in the same room and talk or not talk and it was fine with both of us. I normally went to bed after the news, and she stayed up reading. I couldn't sleep deeply until she came to bed around one o'clock in the morning. I felt her climb into bed and as careful as she tried to be not to disturb me, I felt the bed shake. Every morning about one o'clock after she passed away, I'd be in bed, and would feel the bed shake. Startled, I'd jump up and look over at her side of the bed. Of course, she wasn't there, but I was certain that our bed shook. I stayed in hotels on several occasions because I couldn't stand that bed shaking every night.

I still talk to her from time to time and think she is still here with me in spirit. We were married fifty-one years, but because we played together as children, we were together for over seventy years. I much rather have lost a limb than to have lost her, but she always insisted that I had to have faith and stay positive no matter what happened.

Allen:

I admired my wife very much for her ability to always stay positive. She was an incredibly positive person and encouraged positive things and displayed happiness. She got up in the morning with the attitude that this was going to be a delightful day, and she worked all day to make it that way and make others happy. If you were feeling bad, she pulled you right out of that saying, 'You know, life is good. Enjoy every minute of it.' Even when she was sick, she didn't want to complain because in her mind, she was trusting in God. I admired that, and I worked hard to emulate her, but it wasn't easy. She was like a beautiful butterfly who touched a lot of people's lives in so many positive ways. One thing she loved to do was teach at a Sabbath Day school. She played like she herself was a child and kids loved that *about her. My wife was somebody you could really talk to and that was so special because she helped with any problems I had. She married a big problem, but she talked me through a lot of issues I had concerning my past.*

She was the first one to tell me about Jesus when she was just a little girl, and I had a long way to go to learn all that I did. She could have very well been the turning point that kept me from being an undesirable person. I had so much discontent in my life, and she spent a lot of time being concerned about my feelings. Whenever I was upset about something she said, 'We need to talk about this.' It was just an incredible feeling to have somebody pull you from your darkest place and into a bright light. My gratitude for her is enormous and she is missed in my life in every way imaginable.

Janelle:

We talked a lot during one of my last visits with Mom. I told her how much I loved her and that she was the woman I most admired. I told her I felt like I had won the lottery when God chose her to be my mother and that I would be forever grateful for that win. I told her that if I could even be one-tenth of the mother she was to my own two children, then I will feel like I have done an excellent job. She mouthed the words, 'You're just as good as me and I am so proud of you.' My mother to me was the closest thing to perfection. She achieved this higher state of being and understanding. Because of this, love poured all around her, attracting so many who found her and received her love. I hope in time I get there too and achieve this wonderous state that I know we are all searching for. Her role was crucial for our continuation as a "family unit." When we lost her, I tried to fill her role in the family, but no one could fill her shoes.

Always stating that she had plenty in life, she gave so much to this world and took so little in return.

Travis:

I went to church on Saturdays with my mother and she had the tender heart to take care of us. She was my dad's biggest supporter and made him a much better person because they complemented each other. She wrote notes every morning with a verse from the bible; words of inspiration and love she thought might help me throughout my day. Mom was my person, always protecting me, helping me with homework, making lunches, driving an hour round trip to my private school, and even mapped out personal directions for me when I worked at FedEx so I wouldn't get lost. She was an amazing woman and I dearly miss her presence in my life.

Becky:

Mom was truly kind and gentle with us and loved our family to the extreme. I can picture her wanting to sit down and absorb it all, especially the grandkids. I remember she was always busy because she ran the Pretti-Pet grooming business from home, and had to be stressed with everything going on, plus us kids were everywhere. She managed it so well that you would never have known if she needed a break. I know we put her through it, but she was always there for us. I feel lucky that she was my mom.

Amanda:

It's funny that I have a hugely different perspective now that I am a mom. My parents' house was the one that all my friends came to. I didn't go to their houses; they came to mine because it was a fun place to be. Mom made little pizza burgers, and everyone loved them so much. They were always asking her to make them, even though she thought the recipe was too easy. I never remember her saying, 'Oh no, I don't want everybody in the house!' How did my parents never seem irritated about that? Instead, they encouraged my friends to visit.

In my mother's final days, she became less and less responsive as she slowly made her exit from this world. When someone called, 'Darlene,' she sometimes opened her eyes, but when one of her children said, 'Mom,' she opened her eyes to look at us every single time. It's amazing to me that once we become a mother, that piece of our identity is so unshakable, that it is the last part we are willing to let go of. Even in our last breaths, as we leave the world behind, we still look for our children when they call out, 'Mom.'

Darlene physically left this earth on March 12, 2017, and is survived by her husband, Allen, her four children Janelle, Travis, Rebecca, and Amanda, and six grandchildren, Mitchell, Lilly, Olivia, Caleb, Anabelle, and Violet.

Darlene with children and grandchildren
Photo by Melissa Joy Photography

Left to right: Amanda, Janelle, Travis, Darlene and Rebecca
Photo by Melissa Joy Photography

Grandkids
Left to right: Anabelle, Olivia, Lilly, Caleb, Mitchell and Violet 2022

Have you noticed as you look around, I am not with you,
I am nowhere to be found?

Are you lonesome for the way we used to be?
Do you ever want to be with me?

I have noticed, and it is so hard to bear,
to wake up each morning and find you're not there.

Can it be that you have noticed too, or will I notice
a lifetime without you?

Have you noticed as time passes by, there is no sunshine,
no blue in the sky?

I am so lonesome for the way we used to be.
Darling, do you ever think of me?

I have noticed, and it is so hard to bear. To wake up
each morning and find you are not there.

Can it be that you have noticed too?
Or will I notice a lifetime without you?

–Allen Karl

As one can only imagine, Allen could no longer bear the memories rushing back or enjoy living in the shadows of what used to be. In 2018, he sold the farm, gave nearly everything away, and started over in Murfreesboro, Tennessee. A move which brought him closer to the country music that saved him, and farther away from the pain of all that he lost.

I won't even drive on Johnnycake Road now because the day I left; it was for good. I drove down the driveway, stopped at the end, and just cried like a baby. I left my entire life there that day. All the things I built, the wonderful times we shared-everything. I never expected to live longer than my wife. I was supposed to go first, but it just didn't work out that way. I sometimes wish that someone could simply take away all my memories, because they are slowly killing me.

24

The Good Guy in the Black Hat

"For it isn't your father, your mother, or your wife, whose judgement
upon you must pass, the fellow whose verdict counts most
in your life, is the one staring back from the glass."
–Peter Dale Wimbrow Sr.

When Allen readies himself for a show, he dons his best country music suit with a southwestern flair. His ensemble always includes the 'End of The Trail' turquoise insignia bolo tie and belt buckle, along with his dressy cowboy boots. Staring back at himself in the dressing room mirror framed and brightly lit with globe lights, his eyes gleamed. "We're all set for you, Mr. Karl. You're on in fifteen minutes." Allen carefully places his signature black cowboy hat on his head, runs his fingers along the brim, and smiles genuinely. I can't help but wonder, when he stares back at the man in the glass, is he content with the man that he sees? There's no doubt in my mind that he should be incredibly proud of the person he has become, because he truly is a Country Gentleman, and well deserving of being pinned, "The Good Guy in the Black Hat." Publisher Ruth Reese chimes in:

"When I was a child going to cowboy shows, we always knew who the good guy was because he always wore a white hat. Not so in the music industry, because I know a good guy who wears a black hat. His name is Allen Karl. He has earned the title of "The Good Guy in the Black Hat," because he is one of the nicest guys I have ever met. He always has a big smile and a firm handshake for everyone he meets, and always tries to show his

fans how much he appreciates them. His great personality is down-to-earth, and he makes an impression everywhere he goes."

Sketch by Geoffrey Beadle of the Good Guy in the Black Hat

Bob Everhart continues:

"Country recording artist Allen Karl is much more than "The Good Guy in the Black Hat." He is a seasoned entertainer, international dignitary, and preserver of the traditional country and western music genre that defined a nation. Much has been written about this man and his music, with many phrases used to describe him, most of which fit him to a 'T.' However, a couple of things have been left out of these descriptions and phrases – like his million-dollar smile and those eyes that say to his audience, 'This song is for you,' and that audience knows he means it. It takes a true professional to accomplish this each time he takes to the stage. So, let's add to that phrase, 'The Good Guy

in the Black Hat.' He is sincere, approachable, and a true Country Gentleman. Now, you have the perfect description of Allen Karl."

Allen Karl, as he is known world-wide in the country music industry, has indeed made an impression wherever he goes. His passion for music took him from a beaten down boy receiving a second-hand guitar at the age of twelve, to a highly decorated, confident, and seasoned entertainer at the age of eighty-two. Seventy years of dedication to music and to his fans throughout the world, is the gift this man humbly offers. When everyone and everything is gone, music will be the only thing that stays, and that's why we love it so much. Perhaps that is why Allen loves music so much, too. In fact, Allen's one true love and his true North in life has always been traditional country music. To truly grasp a better understanding of this man, you will need to listen closely to the lyrics he sings. Throughout his lengthy recording career, he never once chose a song to record or perform that didn't resonate with him. For Allen, music has been his lifeline, because over the last seventy years, his audiences from all walks of life, offered him the love and approval he needed to heal on the deepest level. Center stage, in the beam of a spotlight, and in front of thousands is ironically where Allen hid his painful past from the world. His smile, the gleam in his eyes, and his heart-felt deliverance of his songs were the perfect camouflage and cloak. Imagine seventy years of paving your path in life through music. Each stone carefully placed, some pavers more prominent and noticeable than others, and yet they all together weave their way down the path of an enormously successful music career.

The songs that best define Allen Karl include: 'A Lover's Plea,' 'Butterflies,' 'Don't Tell Me Your Troubles,' 'Right or Wrong,' 'Lonelys Only Bar,' 'That Juke Box Has a Mind of Its Own,' 'My Final Rose,' 'Put Another Log on the Fire,' 'As Sure as I'm Standing Here,' 'It's Too

Early to Cry in My Beer,' and 'That's All Behind Me Now.' These are among the over three hundred songs that he has recorded, most of which went platinum, gold, or number one on the independent country music charts. Allen also recorded twenty-nine gospel songs including his all-time favorite, 'Mansion Over the Hilltop,' using his grandfather's restored mandolin which made the song sound even sweeter.

I honestly wish I could tell you how many gold or platinum records I have. I guess I just don't keep a score of my achievements the way I should. My daughter, Amanda, who found all my plaques in boxes when I moved, said, 'Dad, you need to put these all on the wall!' Well, I put many of them on the wall, but I still don't know what all I have.

What Allen has is a life well-lived and an award-winning sound-track to go with it. If you ask Allen, awards don't make the entertainer, but they do help to validate and differentiate an artist. It's true that any legitimate artist understands that awards are absurd, as we all know that some of the world's greatest artists never won awards. The fact is that Allen made it to the very top in one of the toughest businesses in the world and has the accolades to prove it.

"Cherokee Warrior" Donny Young

One of Allen's proudest moments was his induction into the Native American Hall of Fame. Chief Black Eagle of the Cherokee Nation personally inducted him on March 17, 1992. In a proclamation read by the chief, Allen was respectfully dubbed MA'TO-PO-TAN-KA (Bear with a big voice) and became an honorary member of the Cherokee Nation. Chief Black Eagle expressed his deepest gratitude to Allen for being such a good friend to the Native Americans.

In Pennsylvania, North Carolina, and Oklahoma, I performed benefits shows for the Cherokees to raise money for school supplies and medications for their hospitals. Chief Black Eagle designated the End of the Trail as my sign to display at my shows, so I would always have that symbol hanging behind me. The ceremony was held in Pennsylvania, and I was so proud to have my wife there with me for this momentous occasion. We were both so incredibly happy to be there.

No doubt that being inducted into the George D. Hay Foundation Hall of Fame in 2013 was significant in Allen's illustrious music career. This was an honor bestowed upon him in Mammoth Springs, Arkansas alongside Vince Gill, John Hughey, Dallas Frazier, and Larry Sparks. In Nashville, Tennessee, George D. Hay was known for founding The Grand Ole Opry back in 1925. It started as a one-hour 'Barn Dance' on WSM Radio and has grown into the home of country music with members recognized around the globe as the greatest country performers of all-time.[29] Allen gladly entertained the crowd at the induction before having his picture added to the wall of fame. The same photo that graces the cover of this book is now proudly displayed on the wall inside the home of the owner of the foundation. He is in good company hanging there amongst the likes of Marty Robbins, George Jones, Dolly Parton, Roy Acuff, and Gene Autry.

"Dear Mr. Karl, the George D. Hay Foundation has the distinct pleasure to inform you that you have been selected for induction into The George D. Hay Hall of Fame. This Hall of Fame induction by the foundation selection committee recognizes rare individuals who have played an outstanding, enduring role in the world of country music. Your musical history and career set you apart as one such individual."

The European Country Music Association (ECMA) rounds out the top three of Allen's mountain of recognition. Over the years, the BBC Radio aired all of Allen's European concerts backed by the Red River Band, and altogether he won three Outstanding Achievement awards for his songs – 'As Sure as I'm Standing Here,' 'Lonelys Only Bar,' and 'Butterflies.' In 2011, Allen also won Album of the Year for 'My Final Rose' as well as Male Vocalist of the Year. The person who oversaw the ECMA's flew from Spain to London to personally hand Allen his plaques and throw a large party following the ceremony. Allen's song 'Butterflies,' written by Jerry Foster, was choreographed for a line dance in Spain. Invitations went out to line dance to the song, video it, and then send it in for a chance to open for Allen on his next European tour. Five women from Cape Town, South Africa won the contest and subsequently opened for Allen in England.

Allen counts Jim Reeves, Eddy Arnold, Willie Nelson, and Waylon Jennings as his biggest musical influences, but his voice and style are all his own. His drive and tenacity over the years, landed him the spotlight in countless venues all over the world, but his pinnacle performance was given from inside the iconic circle, center stage at the Grand Ole Opry. He then performed during the Opry Gospel Hour as a special guest of Hank Snow.

The following are just a few of Allen's many accolades and honors:

- Outstanding Achievement Award-Sundial Records, Nashville. 1989
- Face of Love with Dottie Snow, (Hank Snow's daughter-in-law). Video of the Year 1991
- Indie Bullet Chart Performance Nominee for Top Male Vocalist, 1991
- Appalachian Jubilee, Inc. Certificate of Merit, 1991
- EIA (The Entertainer Indi-Association Distinguished Achievement) EIA's Most Promising Male Entertainer, 1992
- Texas Hall of Fame, 1995
- Old Time Country Music Hall of Fame, 2008
- Induction into the Iowa Traditional Country Music Hall of Fame, 2008
- Honor from Star Creek Records International Recording Artist, 2009
- Rural Roots Music Commission National Contemporary Country CD of the Year, 2009
- Rural Roots Music Commission National Country DVD of the Year 'My Final Rose,' 2010
- Great Country Radio Award, 2011
- Indie World of Country Music's Top Independent Country Artist of the World, 2011
- Member of the Traditional Country Opera, 2012
- National Independent Artists Hall of Fame Duet of the Year, 2012
- Indie World of Country Music's Top Independent Artist of the World, 2012
- National Independent Artists Hall of Fame Great Country Radio Male Vocalist of the Year, 2012
- The Traditional Country Music Association's Lifetime Achievement Award, 2012

- Wildhorse Entertainment Independent Superstars Recording Artist Hall of Fame for lifetime contributions as a professional recording artist, 2013
- National Independent Artists Hall of Fame, 2013
- Rural Roots Music Commission National Traditional Country Single of the Year, 2013
- Fair Play Country Music Magazine's Label of the Year, Century II Records, 2015
- Indie World of Country Music's Top Artist of the World, 2018
- Indie World of Country Music's Top Independent Country Artist of the World, 2018
- Josie Awards Record Label of the Year-Century II Records, 2018
- The EPCM Most Appreciated Studio Recording Company, 2020
- European Country Association Award for Appreciation of Keepin' It Country, 2021

The following are testimonials pulled from several of Allen's album covers:

"Allen once told me during a particularly insightful conversation that he would never record a song he didn't feel connected to in some way. That's amazing considering the hundreds of tunes that Allen has released over the years. Can one man exude that much genuine emotion? If you know Allen like I do, there's no debating that question. I have met very few like him who are so open, sensitive, and tuned-in to the beauty and creativity around them. Like he sings in the title track of this CD, he is driven by love and desires to always reflect that love for the good of everyone around him. Allen does that best through his wonderful music, which has touched millions of lives around the world. Whether you are a long-time fan of Allen's, or hearing him for the very first time, you will no doubt be delighted and even transformed. If Allen has his way, his music will touch your heart, stir your senses, and inspire you to continue moving forward with confidence on your journey. Thanks be to God for giving us this special, unique, and talented man whose passion for life and love drives us all to be the absolute best that we can be."

–Luanne Hunt

"Allen Karl is the vision of perseverance. The definition of perseverance is one who has continued patient effort to all that he is committed to doing in his life. Since my first introduction to Allen in 2010, I never realized how strong this man was in his belief to make traditional country music his life's dream. He is the true epitome of a loving husband and father, a God-fearing man, honest, and true to his beliefs in life. I have come to know that I am a lucky person to work with this artist. I have worked closely with Johnny Paycheck, Ray Price, and Jerry Reed, and they are all great, legendary artists in country music. Honestly, I have never met or worked with someone who could keep all avenues of his life in proper order and be successful in all these areas. From doing whatever it takes to become known world-wide, by building a bridge of new fans, Allen has garnered an impressive fan base. This man from the Quaker State has shared the stage with such legends as Bill Anderson, John Conlee, Willie Nelson, and so many other artists who have come to also know him as the 'Good Guy in the Black Hat.' I know from my experience with Allen how strongly he believes in honesty, integrity, and a true love of traditional country music. I learned from him that dreaming is a part of his success, and he has applied his great talents to persevere against all odds in a field where there are only a chosen few who reach the pinnacle of the mountain of success. Allen Karl is the lesson in country music that should be written and given to every artist to read and live by in their pursuit of success." –Marty Martel

Irlene Mandrell

You know I enjoyed the music and it's not about the awards, just the music itself. I want to thank all the wonderful people in country music who have encouraged, supported, and inspired me throughout my career. All the wonderful disc jockeys and program directors of country music, my publicist, promoters, and booking agents. The list goes on and on. But most of all, I feel enormous gratitude to my fans. Meeting them at concerts and hearing from them by mail has meant the world to me. My grandfather, whose memory I cherish, had always told me that as I walk down my path in life, I should endeavor to be an encouragement and inspiration to everyone I meet and leave them with the feeling that their life is just a little better because we met. And then he added, 'Allen, if you don't feel that you are doing that, then you must be on the wrong path.' To entertain, encourage, and inspire my fans was most important to me. Just to know that through a song, a handshake, a hug, word, or a smile, I made a small positive difference in someone's life makes me want to say to myself, 'Pop, I think I'm on the right path.' May God bless you, and I thank you all sincerely.

–Allen Karl

When it comes to young talent rising in the business, Allen aspires to be a positive influence like many of the legendary performers he performed with provided for him. Anyone striving to be involved in country music must be certain that the music business is something they love passionately. Focus on your passion, plan it out, and stick to it. In 1987, Allen started Century II Records, LLC which became one of the most trusted and well-recognized independent country music record labels in the world. The label won multiple awards while helping aspiring traditional country music artists to rise to the top and live their dreams one performance at a time.

THE GOOD GUY IN THE BLACK HAT

An Official Big League Trading Card

25

Century II Records, LLC

"Hold on to your dreams with both hands and don't let go.
There's no guarantee you'll make it to the top, but I can promise
you one hell of a ride. And sometimes that can be enough."
–Allen Karl

When Allen's recording contract with Sundial Records ran its course, he started his very own record label in 1987 called Century II Records, LLC. He was the President, CEO, and the first recording artist on the label. His intentions were to produce quality traditional country music that radio disc jockeys around the world would respect and play. Gradually Allen started adding artists to his label with the idea of not charging them a single dime to record, produce, and promote them. This was unheard of in Nashville, or anywhere in the world for that matter. In a business known for gauging people and taking advantage of their pocketbook while holding their dreams hostage, Century II Records' approach was refreshing.

Through Marty Martel, CEO of Midnight Special Productions, Allen was introduced to Donna Cunningham. She signed to the label and became Allen's duet partner and together recorded songs which consistently soared to the top of independent country music charts. Over the last thirty-five years, Century II recording artists have consistently released number one hits, reached gold and platinum status, and have been recognized world-wide. To qualify for platinum status, a song must have two million or more downloads for airplay. Every artist with Century II Records has earned at least one platinum or gold song. Since 1987, Century II recording artists have included: Bobby G. Rice, Jim Ed Brown, Jean Shepard, Jerry Foster, Julie Richardson, Tina Patterson-White, Chuck Hancock, Tammy Kendrick, Wendy Carter, Donna Cunningham, Amberley Beatty, Marty Dunn, Terry Crabtree, Elvis Presley Jr., Rose Angelica, Lacey Snider, Dean Holmen, the Hammond Brothers, Willie Carver, Val Storey, and Kristi Kalyn.

My record label was entirely about preserving traditional country music because I've always loved this genre of music myself. Eddie Arnold, Jim Reeves, Johnny Cash, Hank Snow, and Anne Murray were just a few heroes of mine. The Grand Ole Opry was at the new location next to the Opryland Hotel. I've never performed at The Ryman Auditorium, but when I stood on that sacred wooden circle which came from the Ryman, it felt surreal.

In 1974, wood was cut from the center stage of the historic Ryman Auditorium and placed on the new stage in Opryland. The entire process was done under the watchful eye of Roy Acuff himself and the circle is a special spot in country music today.[30]

When I walked up and stepped inside the circle and behind the microphone to sing in front of the large crowd, it was fantastic. The place was packed, and I saw nothing but faces all over the place. The band started, and as soon as I started singing, I heard a PA system like you couldn't believe. It was just the greatest PA system on which I have ever performed.

Allen travelled to Europe at his own expense, bringing along his road manager, Joe Eder. Joe was a fantastic person and an important figure in Allen's professional life. He did everything to promote Century II Records and was overall, an amazing manager. Joe also ran the popular Allen Karl Radio Show called 'Allen Karl's Country

Allen with Roy Acuff
Grand Ole Opry

Grand Ole Opry
Gospel Hour Performance

Corner.' This radio show boasts over one hundred and twenty-five recorded shows interviewing some of the biggest names in country music. Artists such as Jim Ed Brown, Ronnie McDowell, Helen Cornelius, Stonewall Jackson, and many others. Joe oversaw all the editing; spending hours making everything sound right and cutting each segment to exactly thirty minutes. When he left Century II Records, his presence was missed.

Joe Eder was my road manager who managed all the disc jockeys world-wide, and the admiration they have for us was all because of him. He was to Century II Records an especially important figure and the absolute best man to have out there on the road, because he crafted every plan perfectly. He discussed my rate of pay, the contracts, down payments, and booked flights from one country to another. He had everything so well organized that all I had to worry about was selecting my song material.

He was a big man and a force to reckon with, making him the perfect bodyguard. When we moved through the crowds gathered in the various countries, he kept me safe. We were good friends too and always laughed and enjoyed each other's company along the way. We were on the road together for over a week one time, pulling our equipment trailer. I had something stuck in my teeth and was making a sucking sound with my tongue the way you do trying to get food out of the space between your teeth. After a while of doing this, Joe said to me, 'For God's sake, Allen! Why don't you just take your teeth out and clean them?' I said, 'Joe, my teeth don't come out.' He replied, 'Well Allen, if you don't stop making that damn sucking noise, they're going to come out!' I still laugh aloud when I think of that.

I went out to dinner with Bobby G. Rice and Joe and afterwards, we were all hugging and saying our goodbyes. When it came down to the only two people that hadn't hugged were Bobby and Joe, Bobby looked up at Joe like he would look up to the top of a skyscraper and said, 'Okay Joe. How are we going to do this?'

Left to right: Bobby G. Rice, Joe Eder and Allen

He was especially important to me and to Century II Records, and when he decided to move, it was difficult for me to pick up those pieces. Visiting Joe in Florida before I die is on my bucket list. I want to see him and thank him personally one last time for the things he's done for Century II Records, and for me.

Allen wrote over sixty songs of his own, although he rarely recorded them. There was a great deal of talent out there and so many songs he felt were much better than his to record. The original songs he recorded all did extremely well and disc jockeys around the world made Allen Karl a house-hold name in traditional country music. Allen appreciated these disc jockeys for playing and promoting his music and personally wanted to thank them.

We flew to Denmark, Sweden, the Netherlands, and all over England and Ireland to personally thank the disc jockeys for playing our records. They honestly couldn't believe it. They put huge tables out filled with food where I was being interviewed, and they displayed an American flag behind me. They don't get thanked like that from the major labels. With the majors it is all pushed to the one hundred big radio stations in the United States, and they are all told what they are going to play. You can go from one station to another, and chances are the same song is going to be playing. That's what they do, but the independent artists are just as good, if not better, than anybody on a major label. It is good for them to be played as well and that's what we are all about. Century II Records is still one of the biggest independent labels in the United States with the tagline, 'Keepin' It Country Since 1987.'

As Allen was leaving the radio station in Denmark, he turned on the radio in his car in time to hear its disc jockey, Peter, come on the air and announce, "I just interviewed Allen Karl, a True Country Gentleman." That was one of the highest compliments Allen could hope to receive, and the pinned nickname of Country Gentleman has stuck with him ever since.

Allen built an incredibly large fanbase and in Nashville, he had his very own Allen Karl Fan Club. He set up every year at Fan Fair in Nashville to greet his fans and traditionally his booth sat on the corner of a main aisle and so it was fondly nicknamed, "Allen Karl's Country Corner." His approachability was unmatched, and he never turned down a plea for an autograph or picture. He has an authenticity that draws people to him, and he adores his fans.

Allen shot several music videos over his career and put together three television pilot shows at the North Star Studios in Nashville. He secured the Hall of Fame singer and songwriter, Jerry Foster to introduce him for each show. Jerry was like the "Ed McMahon" of country music as he would say, "And, heeeeeeere's Allen!" The first three shows were done beautifully with co-hosts for each of the shows including, Stonewall Jackson, Bobby G. Rice, and Jan Howard. Rural Free Delivery TV (RFD TV) wanted to air the program next to Marty Stuart's Show.

RFD TV wanted to put my show on next to Marty Stuart and we needed to do forty-nine more shows for which we selected George Jones, Reba McEntire, and a whole line of "A-List" people. Unfortunately, we just couldn't raise the money. It was going to take a million three to do all these shows. The director of Nashville Now, passed away, but his wife believed she could raise the necessary funds through her connections with the Sioux Native Americans. Despite her efforts, she couldn't raise the money and I was left with just three pilot DVDs. Other television shows I was on included the Wolf Spotlight Show in Pennsylvania and The Country Junction Show out of Kentucky, which aired all over the East Coast. I really had a wonderful time doing all of that and met so many wonderful people who became dear friends of mine.

Throughout his career, Allen seized every opportunity to meet, sing with, and develop relationships with some of the greatest entertainers in the country music industry. He fondly remembers time spent with them as some of the best days of his life.

I became good friends with Stonewall Jackson and spent a lot of time with him. He used to love this place in Goodlettsville called Calhoun's and we ate there often. He'd call me up and say, 'Hey Allen, I am buying dinner. How about meeting me at Calhoun's?' He was such a classy guy. With his reputation of being such a famous star, you would think that he would be arrogant, but he never put on airs. He was so down to earth, that you could swear he wasn't anyone special. He was positively a down home, country boy and when people approached the table for autographs or pictures, he'd say, 'Hey, it's no bother.' Whenever he went into the public and was recognized, he always had a smile, shook hands, and said, 'God Bless You!'

Jim Ed Brown signed with Allen and Century II Records after twenty-seven years with RCA Records. The song he recorded called, 'In Style Again,' soared to number one and Allen was lucky enough to be with him at the Grand Ole Opry when he debuted the song to a standing ovation.

To me, Jim Ed was the epitome of a Southern Gentleman. I sang on the Grand Ole Opry as a guest of Hank Snow several times and I met him backstage. I told him how much I loved his song called, 'Three Bells' which he sang with his sisters, and we got to talking. He wanted to know what I was doing in the music business, and we discussed it. Not long after that, I met him again at John A's Restaurant in Music Valley where we sat together and talked for the longest time.

During our conversation, I mentioned my record label and Jim Ed seemed extremely interested in signing. My dear friend Gene Kennedy, CEO of Doorknob Records, helped to arrange a meeting for all of us and Jim Ed agreed to come aboard. I was absolutely thrilled! We signed the contract at his home and sifted through several hundred songs looking for just the right one for him to record. We found 'In Style Again,' and both of us just loved it. The way he sang that song in the studio, just tore us all apart. Bobby Bare was the producer and the song was a huge hit for him. Jim Ed signed the promotional poster to me saying, 'Allen, thank you for giving me a second chance.' Not long after that he went to the hospital with cancer. I went to see him, and he said, 'You know, Allen. I am going to beat this thing!' Unfortunately, he didn't beat his cancer, but I loved every minute I spent with Jim Ed because he truly was a legend.

Jim Ed Brown and Allen standing on the Opry circle

Hall of Fame Artist, Bobby G. Rice has been a Century II recording artist for years and is best known for his hit, 'You Lay So Easy on My Mind.' Bobby G. has done shows with Allen since the 1970s with their most recent appearance together at Loretta Lynn's Ranch in Hurricane Mills, Tennessee. Bobby just marked his fiftieth anniversary of the release of his famous song and to hear him sing it in person is always a real treat.

Bobby G. Rice is an incredibly special friend of mine and we have done some of the same shows since the 1970s. It is always a wonderful experience being with him and I always liked the fact that he has such dry sense of humor. I am so proud to have him on my label and for the friendship that has lasted over fifty years. I congratulate him on the remarkable success of his song, 'You Lay So Easy on My Mind.' I remember when the song came out. What a great song to dance to and such a considerable number one Billboard hit for him.

Allen with Bobby G. Rice and wife Alice   Bobby G. Rice

Hall of Fame singer and songwriter Jerry Foster signed to Century II Records and Allen recorded at least seven original songs of his. Each one climbing to number one on the independent country music charts.

Jerry Foster became a good friend of mine in 2009 while I was making the three pilot television shows at North Star Studios in Nashville. He is a powerful songwriter, writing hits for Jerry Lee Lewis, Sonny and Cher, Charlie Pride, and so many more. Whenever Jerry and his wife Sharon join me for dinner, we have a wonderful time. His smile is infectious, and he is always bubbly and laughing. In my opinion, he and Kris Kristofferson are two of the top writers in the industry. Over the years, I have recorded seven of Jerry's songs which all soared to number one on the charts. I am not sure if it was because I did an excellent job of singing it or because he was the writer, but I'll always consider him one of my dearest friends.

Jerry Foster

After thirty-five years of success in the music business, Allen sold his beloved record label to a long-time friend and traditional country music supporter, Dean Holmen. Allen remains the CEO, making sure that the acquisition goes as smoothly as possible.

It was time to change hands and pull in new blood to continue to get things done for our artists. Plus, it had become difficult for one person to continue to afford to do it my way. Since I founded the company in 1987, numerous independent music labels have come and gone, but I am proud to say that the record label I created is still here, still going strong, and I never want to see it die. It has been my life's work and my pride and joy. The song, 'May the Circle Be Unbroken,' resonates with me because I don't ever want our Century II Records' circle of talent to be broken. The Century II family of artists, and what has been created over the last thirty-five years, I hope will last forever. I know that we've been an inspiration to so many people through the years with the music we have put out there.

26

Statistically Speaking

*"I am not the things my family did, I am not the voices in my head.
I am not the pieces of the brokenness inside. I am light..."*
—India Arie

A llen is now, and always has been, a warrior of the light. However,
this result should never be taken for granted as a foregone
conclusion. Studies have repeatedly proven that the most common
factor in the making of a serial killer is the experience of childhood
trauma, which can be an immensely powerful sculptor of character-
interrupting early brain development and compromising the nervous
and immune systems. FBI agent and author, Robert Ressler, who
played a significant role in the psychological profiling of violent
offenders in the 1970s and often credited with coining the term
"serial killer", shares the following insight:

> *Let me state equivocally that there is no such thing as a person,
> who at the age of thirty-five, suddenly changes from being
> perfectly normal and erupts into total evil, disruptive, and
> murderous behavior. The behaviors that are precursors to
> murder have been present and developing in that person's life
> for a long, long time-since childhood.*[31]

Lack of affection in infancy, along with childhood physical,
sexual, and psychological abuse, can create the perfect storm in
adulthood. Add to this, absolute neglect, and insecure attachment,
and you would bet your very last dime that the chance of evolving

into a positive and functional human being would be zero. Statistically speaking, Allen should be a serial killer, suffering with chronic health issues, depressed, suicidal, or at the very least, a hardened criminal. It is interesting to note that 66 percent of known serial killers, who were studied by the Federal Bureau of Investigation, were raised by a dominant mother, 42 percent were physically abused, 74 percent were psychologically abused, and 29 percent suffered a head trauma.[32] Allen survived physical, psychological, and sexual abuse, along with neglect, insecure attachment, head trauma, and an adulthood filled with toxic stressors. To better understand the impact these events may have had on Allen, he took the ACEs quiz. Ace stands for: Adverse Childhood Experiences.

The ACEs quiz acts as a helpful tool in raising awareness of the potential impact of adverse childhood experiences and is used widely in the juvenile court system. The score is based on ten types of childhood trauma, five are personal and five are related to other family members. Personal childhood trauma includes physical, verbal, and sexual abuse, along with physical and emotional neglect. Family member trauma would address an alcoholic parent, a mother or father who is a victim of domestic violence, a family member diagnosed with mental illness, disappearance of a parent through divorce, death or abandonment, or a parent in jail. You receive one point for each type of trauma experienced, and the higher your ACEs score, the higher your risk of health and social problems. As your score increases, so does the risk of disease, as well as social and emotional problems. Allen answered "Yes" to nine out of ten questions! This is remarkable, because with a score of four or more, the likelihood of chronic pulmonary lung disease increases by 390 percent, depression by 460 percent, and suicide by 1220 percent. Allen's score was twice as high, only answering "No" regarding an alcoholic parent in the household.[33]

It is important that we remember that this quiz is only meant as a guideline. Adverse childhood experiences affect each child differently, and genetic factors do play a key role, because some children are predisposed to be more sensitive to adversity than others. Allen's extremely high score on the ACEs quiz does not mean that developing social, emotional or health problems is inevitable, it simply means that he is at greater risk of developing lasting mental and physical effects. In addition, the quiz doesn't factor in whether there may have been any relationships present to create a buffer between the child and the adversities. It is interesting that the most common factor among children who show resilience is having at least one stable and responsive relationship with a supportive adult.[34]

The one person early on in Allen's life who was stable and supportive was his maternal grandfather, Pop. Although Pop was guilty of not stopping the array of abuse his grandson repeatedly suffered at the hands of his wife and daughter, he offered stability by providing basic needs. Food, water, and shelter are essential to life, but for Allen, it was his music which became as essential to living as the air that he breathed. It was Pop who gifted his first guitar and offered instruction that became one of Allen's most valuable coping mechanisms throughout life. Without music or Pop in his life, it is highly doubtful that Allen would have become the Good Guy in the Black Hat, or the Country Gentleman.

Pop and Allen grilling fish together

Pop was supportive, but Allen was raised in an era when the entire social attitude towards parenting was much different than it is today. Authoritative and strict discipline in the home was the norm and mental health and child advocacy resources were scarce. This was especially true in the rural countryside, where teachers doubled as counselors, and the go-to classroom management techniques included whacks with a ruler, paddle, or chalkboard pointer. Sadly, it wasn't until the 1970s that governmental child abuse prevention agencies gained momentum, which was too late for Allen and Jerry.[35] It certainly would have taken a team of professionals to intercede and turn things around for them.

Today, we recognize that responding to abuse is not a choice, but a requirement, because the repercussions of not acting can have devastating and lifelong effects for children.[36] It is appalling that Allen's entire family, along with his teachers, truancy officers, neighbors, friends, and other community members, ignored what was glaringly evident; these boys were being tortured daily. If they asked Allen directly if he was being "mistreated," and he denied it for fear of retribution, the subject was conveniently dropped. Now "off the hook" for the responsibility of taking action to remove the boys from the situation, the elephant in the room, no longer existed. No one wanted to get involved. They had a responsibility to their own families and didn't want to raise two young boys, or worse yet, place them in an orphanage, splitting the siblings apart. Doing nothing, was doing something back then.

Having a mother who was the greatest actor of all time didn't help matters either. When in the company of others, Kitty was overwhelmingly convincing that she was the best mother in the world. Her outgoing, loving, and jovial personality would throw the scent off even the best tracking hound. No one expected this woman to be an abuser – a mother of two, and a well-liked socialite. As she entertained, friends and family gushed to Allen how "lucky" he was to have such a wonderful mother. Imagine the psychological pain those comments inflicted and how it added to the feelings of helplessness. No one would have believed the boy and taken his word over his mother or grandmother. When the last guest waved goodbye, and the door closed, the demon inside Kitty emerged and the boys scrambled to accommodate her every demand. She was the epitome of a Jekyll and Hyde. There was no other choice than to appease their mother and stall for time. Nothing short of amazing-the mental strength he mustered to "play her game" and withstand a hostile environment. Allen possessed a strong will to live, and he honestly believed that one day, it would all finally end, and it did.

Thankfully, the childhood adversities did end, but as an adult, Allen faced some difficult challenges. If there was a silver-lining in suffering such a cruel upbringing, it was that his childhood molded him into a highly resilient man. In fact, very few can develop this ultimate level of resilience in their life. Being resilient means possessing the ability to overcome serious hardships and continue to function well, despite the challenges-often coming back stronger than before.[37] Highly resilient people like Allen, find a way to change course, overcome, forgive, emotionally heal, and continue to move forward to accomplish their goals. He is highly resilient, but his soul is not completely unscathed, perfect, or without a glitch. The fact that he turned out to be such a loving, forgiving, generous, and good human being, when he could have easily turned out bitter and violent, has us all scratching our heads in amazement. How is it possible that Allen crushed the odds? Not just with little to spare, but by a million miles? The answer is found in his self-prescribed coping mechanisms.

Coping mechanisms are cognitive and behavioral approaches that we use to manage internal and external stressors.[38] When Allen couldn't control his external world, he turned within and mastered his mind. He created a loving and supportive relationship with God, through Harvey, and found solace and comfort sitting with him alongside a stream. Allen created safe and happy places in his mind to escape to.

I can't say that I didn't need counseling, but I can say with total confidence that I didn't get it. It is hard to say how I got beyond what others may have a tough time getting beyond. While I was being mistreated as a child, I found a place in my mind where I could go, and it was a happy place. It was a place where I felt protected, and I had to think about that place, despite feeling the real pain of a beating or while being sexually violated. I designated a place in my mind where I could go and survive for that day, although I was certain that tomorrow would bring another beating. I had to be determined and focused, because I was alone, and I only had control over my thoughts. I had to think the most positive thing possible and that is how I walked through life. Without this ability to escape in your mind, you're lost. Those that don't make it, are those that give up mentally. They give into the darkness, and you can never give up on yourself. I never entertained the thought of hurting anyone or becoming anything like a serial killer. All I wanted to do was live-to survive. I just wanted to take the beatings and then go off on my own down to the stream. I screamed out, to the top of my lungs, in those woods. I cried out, 'God, help me!' It was by a rippling stream surrounded by nature, that I felt Harvey's presence the strongest. Harvey was so important to me, and I remember always being overly concerned about Harvey's well-being, because he took those beatings along with me. I couldn't lose Harvey. He was my beacon of light in the darkness and one of my greatest coping mechanisms.

Interacting with Harvey, spending time with animals outside in nature, and creating places in his mind that were safe and happy, were all self-prescribed ways to cope with reality. The most effective and long lasting of Allen's coping mechanisms would come in the form of music. Being able to express himself in song and lose himself in a melody is still to this day, Allen's largest life buoy. Without music, Allen would not have had the opportunity to break free from the total lockdown and shut out his mother created at home. Radio shows and live performances as a teenager, provided the adoration of fans and the approval of large audiences. The approval of the masses was the medicine needed most to start healing the gaping emotional and psychological wounds. His talent was recognized and encouraged by some of the most successful people in the industry and their inclusion and encouragement fueled a life-long, significant career.

As an adult, Allen found the love and affection of a good woman, who stuck by him through the roughest waves of adversity. Darlene loved Allen and believed in him. She proudly told others that her husband could fall into a cesspool and come out wearing a Rolex watch. She knew he worked best under pressure, and she placed utmost faith in him. It was her conviction that helping others was the key to absolute happiness, which gave Allen his additional coping strategy. He dedicated his life to helping others and most recently, to helping aspiring country music artists realize their dreams. Allen has granted countless thousands of dollars, through Century II Records, to ensure that dreamers wouldn't be taken advantage of in the jungle of the Nashville music industry.

The golden thread of coping mechanisms throughout Allen's life has always been hard work. Allen is a perfectionist and accepts nothing less than his absolute best effort in everything he does, and he copes with adversity by staying active. Even at the age of eighty-two, naps are never an option. His master carpentry skills create some of the finest items from raised gardens, fences, gorgeous decks, workshop benches and more. His yard is filled with flowering bushes, hanging baskets, and a lawn carpet-like in appearance. You will never find him idle, as he moves from one project to another, but keeping busy is his secret to staying young and freeing his mind from the past. As his neighbor and dear friend Troy Festervand puts it, "If Allen is home, he is working. Daylight until dark, inside the house or outside, it doesn't matter. How can a man his age work as long and hard as he does? We often talk about philosophical issues. When he speaks, it is about the beauty of life. It is rare that a negative word passes his lips. Quiet, respectful, and kind, Allen's world is music and family. I consider myself lucky to know him and call him my friend!"

Troy and Carolyn Festervand, Julie Richardson and Allen

Allen never realized while growing up that turning out to be a good person was a choice. Unaware the odds were stacked against him, he inadvertently chose to be and do better, because anything else was unimaginable. He shattered the cycle of violence in his own family and was self-driven to be the best husband, father, and grandfather possible. Allen made the conscious choice to not allow his past to negatively define him or render him a victim. The best lessons in life are drawn from what not to do. If that is the case, then Allen had the most highly qualified teacher in the world-his mother. At this stage of his life, he has an advantage over most, because he is used to getting through challenging times. If you ask Allen what his recipe for surviving and thriving is, he flashes his signature boyish smile and simply says, "It was Harvey, music, a determined mind, and a strong work ethic, that made the defining differences in my life."

A Resilient Man

27

Not Over It, but Through It

*"It takes a lot of strength and courage to put the past behind you
and stand up and say: 'I will not let it define me.' To push
forward and create the life that you truly deserve and
not focus on bad things that life handed you in the past."*
—Positive Outlooks Blog

Allen and his baby brother, Jerry certainly lived through hell as children, and as a result were robbed of the most important part of their lives. It would be understandable if they adopted the motto: "Life's a bitch and then you die." Instead, they discovered light and goodness in life by adopting resilience, persevering, and being better than the ones that hurt them. Developing a one-on-one relationship with God along the way also helped to make sure that wickedness didn't win. Jerry reflects:

*People I've talked to over the years ask me, 'Why aren't you on
skid row? Why didn't you retaliate? Why didn't you say, well, if
I'm treated this way, I'm going to beat the heck out of my kids
too?' I never laid a hand on my kids, and I never once attempted
to hit my wife, Martha, in over fifty years of marriage. I never
will. I don't honestly know why I didn't turn out differently. I
have more of a love for people and have more patience than
most. The Lord led me to the work that I did in public relations,
marketing, and in helping people in general. I felt like the devil
wanted me to be more like my mother, but the Lord had more
power over me than I thought He would. I was drafted into the*

Army and that was an exceedingly challenging time for me because I had no self-esteem or social skills. I was beaten down so badly, and I wondered how I was going to deal with being in the Army. I didn't have any experience. I was never in the Boy Scouts, I never went camping with a group, and I never played sports or understood teamwork. I was thrown into it with drill sergeants calling me everything under the sun. How am I going to react to that? But I did it! I served four years total with two years served in Vietnam, and they honored me with a Bronze Star. It was like being caged up for years and then told to get out there and fend for yourself.

I was locked up for twenty years and then thrown out into the world. I could have easily gone from the frying pan into the fire. I could have easily said to myself, 'There is no way I'm going to take a chance on another woman, because I already lived with one for twenty years. I am going to remain single with no commitments, forever.' I should be committed; I should have lost it a long time ago. I really don't know how physically, mentally, and emotionally we've been able to maintain our sanity, and never went to counseling. I just took it one day at a time.

To anyone that believes they are in a situation that's not "normal," where they aren't being treated the way they should be, please get help. Talk to anyone that is empowered to act, because it can help the situation. The question remains: how will you know what is not "normal?" That's what Allen and I struggled with because we couldn't understand why we were being treated so poorly. We were not bad kids at all. It is especially important to be willing to seek the help that you need. If you don't get that help from one person, then ask someone else, and don't give up trying to get someone to listen. Use the resources available to your advantage because they certainly didn't exist when we were growing up.

Allen never got over the events of his past, but he plowed his way through them one at a time using his inner strength and believes with all his heart that you can too.

There is so much adversity in life and you are going to run into walls. It may seem hopeless at the time, but you must get through it no matter what it takes. Make it happen. I have had so many disappointments like completely losing businesses and not having any money, and I always had to come back. I couldn't go to somebody and say, 'Hey I just lost my business. It got washed down the river for a second time and we have a second mortgage on our home and kids to raise. Tell me how I am going to do this?' I just never did that. Yet, I had to make it happen. It was always up to me to make it happen, and I couldn't share that with a psychologist. I don't know what they could tell me that would "fix" it. Other than if they were going to give me money to get myself back in business, what are you going to do for me? How could they ever relate? I had nobody to depend on but me and I had to protect my little brother because he depended on me too. Later in life, my wife, four children, and my employees all depended on me. I was forced to develop an inner strength to get me the heck through it; and that's the way it has been my entire life. You must tell yourself no matter how hard it is, or how hard it gets, 'I'm going to make it!' You can't be afraid or timid, just have confidence in yourself.

If you are being mistreated and it's an unbearable situation, which most of the time it is, you need to pull on your inner strength to get through it. Don't give up on it, and whatever you do, don't give in. Giving in means that you've lost, and you can't lose. The key is, you must be strong in your mind, especially when you can't fight back physically. You have a good mind, so use it! Fight with all that you have of your mind and put yourself in another place, giving yourself a mental timeout. Just thinking of existing in another place, even if it's for five minutes, revives you and enables you to go through terrible things. One day, it will be over. It won't last forever, but don't give up on yourself. Sometimes, you are all you've got-let that be enough.

I think back on my childhood and not once in all those years of pure torture, did I ever entertain taking my own life. Even in my adulthood, suicide was never considered to be a viable option for me. I wondered why I didn't think about it as a kid because suicide was the one way I could have instantly escaped. The only answer is that I was headstrong on living. I had to make it through and that's all there was to it. What is it about me that I just can't give up? I can't cry Uncle; I can't do it! Whatever the reason, I kept trudging and that made all the difference in the world. It's been quite a road, both smooth and bumpy. I don't know how much road is ahead of me, but I am willing to find out. I am certainly not going to hide in a closet, I am going to continue to live life to the fullest. I've always told people that life is like walking through a field with these big mud holes. You fall into a mud hole, but you must get out of it and keep going. Then you're walking carefully and yet you fall into another mud hole. The important thing is that you keep getting out of those mud holes because that is the main thing. Don't sit there and cry that you're in that mud hole, get your butt out of there and move forward. And that's it! That's life! I've certainly had my share of mud holes, but I have also had my share of happiness. I've been truly blessed. Keep that cheerful outlook and always remember throughout life, you'll have the chance to pull other people up with you. Don't hesitate, just grab them by the hand and pull! You have the same strength inside of you as I do. If I can do it, you can too!

We can all grasp not getting over a traumatic childhood and recognize that mustering the inner strength to move beyond it is genuinely inspirational. I suppose what trips me up the most at this point is comprehending how Allen was able to forgive his mother. My head is swimming with questions. How is it that he could have anything to do with her once he finally escaped her pull? Paying her bills, hosting her wedding, allowing his children to visit her, feeling remorse for making her cry, and not telling her that he loved her the night she died? It would have been so tempting to harm his mother knowing that it was justified. How could Allen and Jerry both manage to stay the path of goodness while being hit with wave after tidal wave of hate and abuse? My only idea is that they both have a strong internal, moral compass guiding them.

I have come to believe that there exists a moral compass inside us all, but I waiver as to whether we are born with it. Do humans, from the very beginning, have an inherent sense of what is right or wrong, which serves as our "True North?" Or is our internal compass in need of constant calibration as we meet challenges head on and soak up life's lessons? My conclusion is that it is both theories. Humans are born to be good and as we traverse the difficulties of life; we continually calibrate our internal moral compasses to compensate for environmental interferences. If you are not sure who you are, then the process of reduction of who you are not, will eventually bring you to the answer. The best lessons in life are derived from what not to be and Allen was certainly inundated with "what not to be" lessons. I'd like to believe that Allen evolved to a higher level than most and calibrated his internal compass with each traumatic event using it to guide him toward the light-deciding time after time to take the high road of forgiveness. If you choose to do unto others as they have done to you, then you are no better than they are. Jerry adds:

When you are beaten as much as we were, isolated and treated as horribly as us, it wouldn't surprise me if anyone could believe even half of what we said. If I had caused my mother's death, in a court of law, they may have said that it was all justified. In my heart of hearts, I really thought about pouring dirt in that hole while my mother was down there. I was thinking of pushing her down the steps, but I never did. I know something deeper and more profound than I was holding me back, saying to me, 'Don't do it.' It was certainly justified to a point, but I realized that it wasn't ever justified to kill someone. You just have to hang in there because better days are ahead. It's hard to believe that better days are ahead when you're just a young kid, and you are being dragged halfway around the house by your hair and crying your eyes out. You go to bed crying and wake up bemoaning the fact that you have to face another day. It's not worth it and it wasn't hard to pinpoint what the right or wrong thing to do was. If Mom died, it certainly would have been the end of our torment – our being imprisoned and trapped. The physical hurting would disappear, but I am sure the emotional hurt would have done me in. I thought seriously about just giving her a little push. It wouldn't take much, just a little bump and then shut the door and wait for the ambulance to get there. Just say, 'Mom fell down the steps.' Sigh, but I would have to live with that. The Lord said, 'Jerry, don't do it. You're going to survive, and you are going to be a much better person for having gone through it and I am going to help you.' Based on how badly we were treated, I am sure our Lord would have forgiven us, but it would be harder for me emotionally to live with knowing I took a human life.

Allen with Jerry and his wife Martha

To be free to heal your soul from adversities, you must first change the course of action intending to break the cycle of violence-then learn to forgive others. You will need to forgive yourself as well and be kind in your self-talk. Then peace will come dropping slow.

I've been through so much and now it's time for peace. I just need peace in my life, like the poem Desiderata says, which is like a religion for me. Desiderata advises us to keep peace in our souls, be cheerful, and strive to be happy. For me, that says it all. My next chapter in life is upon me now, and I don't know what I need to do, other than continue to live each day striving for happiness. I can't base my success on what happened yesterday. Today is a new day and I hope to wake up in the morning and conduct myself in a way that is better than before. In the end, I just want someone to say, 'He was a nice guy, he loved his family, and he left the earth better for having been here.' In life, music meant so much to me, but when I am no longer able to sing, more than likely, no one will remember me for my music.

Music will come and go, but the love I gave in this world will last forever. By reading my life story, I hope you feel as if you have been on a journey with me, experiencing my highs and lows-laughing and crying. When the last page is turned, I want you to set my book down and smile because you've come to realize that there is still goodness in people despite their pasts. Your past doesn't make you a victim, it doesn't have to define you, nor does it have to hold your future hostage.

Afterword

"Behind you all your memories, before you all your dreams,
around you all who love you, within you all you need."
–Teal Ivy

As a country music artist, myself, I have stood in the wings backstage while the emcee boasts about my accolades and achievements to convince the audience that my upcoming performance will be worth their time and money. My face is void of emotion and my thoughts are far away. I peer out at the band and catch a glimpse of the curtain of brilliant light concealing the vast audience sitting in wait just beyond the stage. Butterflies force a final clearing of my throat as I realize that the very moment I step out into the spotlight, all eyes will fall upon me with unforgiving judgement. The music starts with a countdown from the drummer, queuing my entrance onto the stage. The split-second before the entire auditorium sees me, my entire demeanor changes, and I morph into what everyone came to see – a star. Smiling, waving, confident and deliberate in my moves, as I pour out my soul to strangers chasing that elusive standing ovation. While I sing, I desperately scan the seats for a smile or toes tapping as a hint that I am doing a good job. My last note of each song is held onto like a dear departing friend until applause alleviates any fears I harbored of disapproval. Actress Sally Fields' Oscar acceptance speech comes to mind when she exclaimed, "I can't deny the fact that you like me, right now, you like me!" The idea that people like my singing is the foundation for this addiction of having to perform in front of a live audience. Any approval feeds my ego, and I need that to silence all my ranting self-doubts.

I envision every one of you nodding with affirmation right now because all of us can relate to the necessity to "perform" for others. As humans, we have this insatiable desire to judge others, but crumble at the thought of anyone judging us. That is the very reason we put on a smile, tell people we are okay, and stash away our dreams of someday being our true selves. Our lives are nothing more than daily performances in search of approval from those who judge us. We change who we are to fit the expectation of others, desperately looking for those hints out there that we are doing a "good" job. We secretly carry the troubles that we bear, but the high price we pay for that confidentiality is our own happiness. We do this, because in the end, we just want to be loved. What a wonderful planet this would be if we could all experience unconditional love for being our own unique selves and nothing more.

Allen has spent his entire life performing and hiding the trauma of his childhood abuse behind his famous smile. As Allen wrote in his song, 'Don't Tell Me Your Troubles,' 'My smile prevents them from knowing the score.' Isn't that so true? A smile can hide a warehouse of personal baggage, and if Allen kept smiling and kept pleasing, no one would ever know the brutality this gentle soul has endured. For decades now, Allen has flawlessly played whatever role we each selfishly needed him to play. Maintaining peace was essential to healing his soul wounds but playing these roles for so long ultimately resulted in the sacrifice of his own true happiness and the inability to recognize his authentic self.

I admit that I was surprised the afternoon Allen called me unexpectedly asking me to write his life story. He felt the time was right and hoped to help people by sharing the stories of how he overcame what he went through. I agreed to be his biographer without fully understanding the impact the process would have on me. The man I thought I knew through years in the music industry, was not the same man I have come to know today. I honestly never realized the depth of Allen's goodness, nor his matchless resilience and transcendent level of forgiveness. During our interviews, Allen confided in me with a level of trust that absolutely blew my mind and by doing so, gave me the greatest compliment of my life. I marveled at his bold courage to lower the mask and publish his skeletons in the closet with the sole purpose of helping others. Risking ridicule and judgement in a final effort to discover his authentic self and to know true love. Would people still love him if they knew the real Allen Karl Sterner?

I am not sure if I could ever be brave enough to live my life being true to myself; or stand in that circle of random strangers, arm in arm, allowing the façade of "I am fine, thank you." crumble away and tell all. I don't know if I can tell you who the woman in the glass is just yet, but I do know that if I erased all the mistakes of my past, I wouldn't be wiser today for the lessons that I have learned along the way. You know, Allen asked me to consider time travel for a moment and tell him what year I would travel back to and why. I thought for a moment before replying that I would like to travel back to June 10, 1944 and find that little boy wishing for a birthday cake. I would scoop him up and carry him far away where he'd have the chance at a childhood with a loving mother and father. Smiling proudly, I said, "Then Allen, you wouldn't have experienced so much pain."

Without hesitation, Allen then shared that he would travel back to the 1800s and be a wagon master. Just like the character Ward Bond played on the 1960s TV series, 'Wagon Train.' Ward Bond played the role of a tough, but good-hearted leader who helped pioneers traverse the perilous journey from post-Civil War Missouri to California.[39] I could certainly understand how he could relate to wanting to guide people safely along their journey in search of a better life. It occurred to me that he was already doing that now. He is a modern-day Ward Bond helping others along their journey in search of healing and self-love.

On second thought, time travel is one trip I wouldn't want to take. Although I will never understand why one man had to endure so much pain and heartache throughout his lifetime, I wouldn't want to change even one second. The awe-inspiring person Allen is today, is the culmination of all the events of his past-both good and bad. If sharing his life story can help just one person, then I know Allen will believe it was all worthwhile and my work made a difference too. In retrospect, even if I had the ability to, I wouldn't change one single brushstroke of the masterpiece of a man that Allen Karl Sterner has become.

Julie and Allen backstage at the Troubadour
Theater in Music Valley, Tennessee

Allen, thank you for giving me the rare opportunity to tell your story. I appreciate your faith and trust in me to do so with compassion and integrity. Throughout this journey together, you have taught me a great deal about mental strength, resilience, forgiveness, and love. I have come to know you well and I can say without reservation, you are truly awe inspiring.

I also know that your lifelong dream is to live out your final days in a quaint log cabin on Moosehead Lake near Greenville, Maine. I envision you sitting on that rustic front porch with a stubbled beard, plaid shirt, and Cody, your pet black bear, by your side. Inside there is a crackling warm fire, Sopa de Res on the stove, and Marco Antonio Solis playing on your stereo.

More than anything, I want that dream to come true for you because I know you're a mountain man at heart with a kind soul recharged by nature. All my best to you now and forever.

Love, Julie

The Man in the Glass
originally written in 1934 by (Peter) Dale Wimbrow Sr.

When you get what you want in your struggle for self, and the world makes you King for the day, just go to the mirror, and look at yourself, and see what that man has to say.

For it isn't your father, your mother, or your wife, whose judgement upon you must pass, the person whose verdict counts most in your life, is the one staring back from the glass.

Some people might think you're a straight-shooting chum, and call you a wonderful guy, but the man in the glass says you're only a bum, if you can't look him straight in the eye.

He's the person to please, never mind all the rest, for he's with you clear up to the end, and you've passed your most dangerous, difficult test, if the guy in the glass is your friend.

You may fool the entire world down the pathway of years, and get pats on your back as you pass, but your final reward will be heartaches and tears, if you've cheated the man in the glass.

Desiderata

Go placidly amid the noise and the haste and remember what peace there may be in silence. As far as possible, without surrender, be on good terms with all persons. Speak your truth quietly and clearly; and listen to others, even to the dull and ignorant; they too have their story. Avoid loud and aggressive persons; they are vexatious to the spirit. If you compare yourself with others, you may become vain or bitter, for always there will be greater and lesser persons than yourself. Enjoy your achievements as well as your plans. Keep interested in your own career, however humble; it is a real possession in the changing fortunes of time. Exercise caution in your business affairs, for the world is full of trickery. But let this not blind you to what virtue there is; many persons strive for high ideals, and everywhere life is full of heroism. Be yourself. Especially do not feign affection. Neither be cynical about love; for in the face of all aridity and disenchantment it is perennial as the grass. Take kindly the counsel of the years, gracefully surrendering the things of youth. Nurture strength of spirit to shield you in sudden misfortune. But do not distress yourself with dark imaginings. Many fears are born of fatigue and loneliness. Beyond a wholesome discipline, be gentle with yourself. You are a child of the universe no less than the trees and the stars; you have a right to be here. And whether it is clear to you, no doubt the universe is unfolding as it should. Therefore, be at peace with God, whatever you conceive *Him* to be. And whatever your labors and aspirations, in the noisy confusion of life, keep peace in your soul. With all its shams, drudgery, and broken dreams, it is still a beautiful world. Be cheerful. Strive to be happy.

–Max Ehrmann, 1948

Professor Geoffrey Beadle – Artist

Born in 1970, Geoffrey Beadle is a native of Pottsville, Pennsylvania. An aspiring artist from an early age, he earned his B.F.A. degree in Painting from Temple University's Tyler School of Art in 1995, followed by his M.F.A. in Painting from Boston University in 1997. Beadle has exhibited his drawings and paintings nationwide at venues including the Corvallis Art Center in Corvallis, Oregon, the State Museum of Pennsylvania in Harrisburg, Manifest Gallery in Cincinnati, Limner Gallery in New York, and the Aurora Public Art Commission in Chicago. Beadle has taught at Edinboro University in northwest Pennsylvania since 1999, where he serves as a Professor of Painting and Drawing. He lives in the city of Erie with his wife and two sons and works in a studio adjacent to his home.

The following pages present Geoffrey's art in full detail.

Notes

1. SickKids Staff. (2009, October 18). *Baby's First Breaths.* https://Aboutkidshealth.ca/
2. Almanac. (Accessed 2021, September 1). *Weather History for Pottsville, PA.* Weather History Archive: Historical Weather Data by Date | The Old Farmer's Almanac
3. Ervin, White, (Accessed 2021, August 8). *Gemini Child: Personality Traits and Characteristics.* Gemini Child: Personality Traits and Characteristics (zodiacsigns-horoscope.com)
4. Millman, Dan. (1993) *The Life You Were Born to Live.* Tiburon, California, HJ Kramer Inc., p. 183-188.
5. Grand Voyage Italy. (2014-2022) *Italian Americans: The History of Immigration to America.* https://www.grandvoyageitaly.com/history/italian-americans-the-history-of-immigration-to-america.
6. History.com Editors. (Accessed 2022, July 13). *World War I.* https://History.com/topics/world-war-i/world-war-i-history/
7. Wikipedia Contributors. (Accessed 2021 November 3) *Pottsville, Pennsylvania.*: https://en.wikipedia.org/w/index.php?title=Pottsville,_Pennsylvania&oldid=1119160364
8. Wikipedia Contributors. (Accessed 2021 November 3) *Pottsville, Pennsylvania,* https://en.wikipedia.org/w/index.php?title=Pottsville,_Pennsylvania&oldid=1119160364
9. American Towns Media Contributors. (Accessed 2021, November 3). *The Pottsville Third Brigade Band.* The Pottsville Third Brigade Band – Pottsville, PA (americantowns.com)
10. Greenwald, Morgan. (2019, May 7) *This Is How Parenting Has Changed Since The 1950's.* This Is How Parenting Has Changed Since the 1950s – Best Life (bestlifeonline.com)
11. Wikipedia Contributors. (Accessed 2021, November 3). *Harvey (1950 film).* Harvey (1950 film) – Wikipedia

12. Think Baby Names Contributors. (Accessed 2021, November 3). *What Does Harvey Mean?* Harvey – Name Meaning, what does Harvey mean? (thinkbabynames.com)

13. Hamari Web Contributors (Accessed 2021, September 3). *Harvey Name Meaning in English.* https://hamariweb.com/names/christian/english/boy/harvey-meaning

14. Goodman, Eida. (2019, January 7). *Harvey Name Meaning: Its Powerful Symbolism, Destiny, and Luck: The name Harvey evokes sociability, humility, and sincerity.* Harvey Name Meaning: Its Powerful Symbolism, Destiny, and Luck (nameecho.com)

15. Smyth, Dolores. (2020, January 31). *What is the Biblical Significance of the Number Seven?* What Is the Biblical Significance of the Number 7? (christianity.com)

16. Homesteading, Original (2021, May 24). *Fels Naptha Soap: Here's What It is & How to Use It!* Fels Naptha Soap: Here's What It is & How to Use It! (originalhomesteading.com)

17. Good Reads. (Accessed 2022, November 5). *Plato Quotables* Quote by Plato: "Your silence gives consent." (goodreads.com)

18. Streep. Peg. (2013, October 16). *What Makes a Good Mother Anyway? Why what you don't do matters more than what you do.* What Makes a Good Mother Anyway? | Psychology Today

19. Stanek, Becca. (2022, January 28). *Sociopath Vs. Psychopath: What's the Difference?* Sociopath vs. Psychopath: What's The Difference? – Forbes Health

20. Japan Guide Contributors. (2022, June 18). *Climbing Mount Fuji.* Climbing Mount Fuji (japan-guide.com)

21. In History, Sophia. (2022, May 18). *Karate: It's Ancient Origin and Evolving History.* Karate – Its Ancient Origin and Evolving History (karatephilosophy.com)

22. Wikipedia Contributors. (Accessed 2022, October 1) *Voice of Prophecy.* Voice of Prophecy – Wikipedia

23. Operation Military Kids Contributors. (2022. July 30). *Bronze Star Meaning: 7 Things to Know About This Military*

Medal. https://www.operationmilitarykids.org/bronze-star-meaning

24. Encyclopedia Britannica Contributors. (Accessed 2021, June 5). The Purple Heart. Victoria Cross | British military decoration | Britannica

25. Ross, Theo A. (Accessed 2022, September 3). *History of the Independent Order of the Odd Fellows.* (History – Independent Order of Odd Fellows (odd-fellows.org)

26. This statement was taken from a conversation I had with singer/songwriter Brian Hedges of Tennessee. These are lyric ideas for a future song of his. He's an amazing artist. Check him out on Facebook. Brian Hedges | Facebook

27. Revive, Detox Contributors. (2020, June 18). *Trap Houses – A Thorn in The Fight Against Drug Abuse and Addiction.* Trap Houses – A Thorn in the Fight Against Drug Abuse and Addiction (revivedetoxlosangeles.com)

28. The Palm Beach Institute. (Accessed 2022, August 19). *What Percentage of Alcoholics Recover? Alcoholism Statistics.* What Percentage of Alcoholics Recover? Alcoholism Statistics | PBI (pbinstitute.com)

29. Website Contributors. (Accessed 2022, July 13). *The Grand Ole Opry History.* https://www.opry.com/history/

30. Opry Website Contributors. (2019, May 20). *The History of the Grand Ole Opry's Iconic Circle of Wood.* https://www.opry.com/story/the-history-of-the-grand-ole-opry-s-iconic-circle-of-wood

31. Ressler, Robert. (Accessed 2021, December 7). *Robert Ressler Quotes: Good Reads.* Robert K. Ressler Quotes (Author of *Whoever Fights Monsters*) (goodreads.com)

32. Lehnardt, Karin. (2016, December 30). *56 Interesting Serial Killer Facts.* 56 Unusual Serial Killer Facts | FactRetriever.com *Childhood Trauma as The Biggest Drive of Serial Killers.* (2021, April 19). Writing Bros. Retrieved July 27, 2022, from https://writingbros.com/essay-examples/childhood-trauma-as-the-biggest-drive-of-serial-killers/

33. Shonkoff, Jack P. (2015, March 2). *Take the ACEs Quiz and Learn What It Does and Doesn't Mean*. Take the ACE Quiz – And Learn What It Does and Doesn't Mean – Center on the Developing Child at Harvard University/

34. Masten, Ann S. and Barnes, Andrew J. (2018, July 17). *Resilience in Children: Developmental Perspectives*. Resilience in Children: Developmental Perspectives - PMC (nih.gov)

35. Wikipedia Contributors. (Access 2022, April 5). *Child Protective Services*. https://www.en-wikipedia.org/wiki/child_protective_services/

36. Psychology Today Staff. (2021, December 2). *Child Abuse*. https://www.psychologytoday.com/us/conditions/child-abuse/

37. Psychology Today Contributors. (Accessed 2021, November 5). *Definition of Resilience*. https://www.psychologytoday.com/us/basics/resilience

38. Algorani, Emad B. and Gupta, Vikas. (2022, April 28). *Coping Mechanisms*. https://www.pubmed.ncbi.nlmnih.gov/32644457

39. Wikipedia Contributors. (Access 2021, May 10). *Wagon Train & Ward Bond*. https://en.wikipedia.org/wiki/Wagon_Train

JULIE RICHARDSON is the national award-winning author of *John A. Hobbs: The Life and Times of Music Valley's Visionary.* A Colorado native, Julie earned her bachelor's degree from the University of Colorado at Boulder and completed her graduate work at Metro State University of Denver. Her background is multifarious with teaching, business ownership, travel, therapeutic horsemanship, and professional singing.

Julie first met Allen Karl in 2009, and over the years, they ran in many of the same music circles in Nashville, Tennessee. In 2018, Allen signed her to Century II Records and promoted her music world-wide. Under his direction, Julie became an award-winning, multi-platinum, country music artist with fans enjoying her talent throughout the world.

Inspired by Allen's resilience and indomitable spirit, and drawn to his sincerity and gentleness, Julie was moved to write this biography. The words nestled on these pages recount the untold life story of a brutalized little boy, who against all odds lived to become a true Country Gentleman.

Countless hours of candid interviews reveal this captivating life story of one of traditional country music's most beloved and decorated entertainers. This is not just the story of a celebrity's achievements; it is one of the magnificent resilience of the human spirit.

Brutally abused as a child, Allen discovers his internal strengths and develops his own coping mechanisms to beat the odds, shatter the cycle of abuse, and emerge as a true Country Gentleman.

In this jaw-dropping biography, Allen offers you a rare glimpse into his personal life through the wide-open windows of his soul. His emotional personal accounts, anecdotes, and insights will bring tears, laughter, and a sense of hope. There is power in love and forgiveness and there is light in a world of darkness.

When you turn the final page, you might be compelled to read Allen's story all over again. A treasured addition to your library for years to come and a golden thread that will change your life forever.

Contact Julie via e-mail at www.julierichardson1111@gmail.com, or visit her music website at www.julierichardsonmusic.com

You can purchase additional copies of this book at www.allenkarl.com or by contacting the publisher directly.

To Darlene,

Thank you for loving me and for showing me how to love. You stood by me through all the terrible times and proved you were always there for me. I've loved you with all my heart, and God knows I would have taken care of you until the day that I died.

With loving memories,

Allen

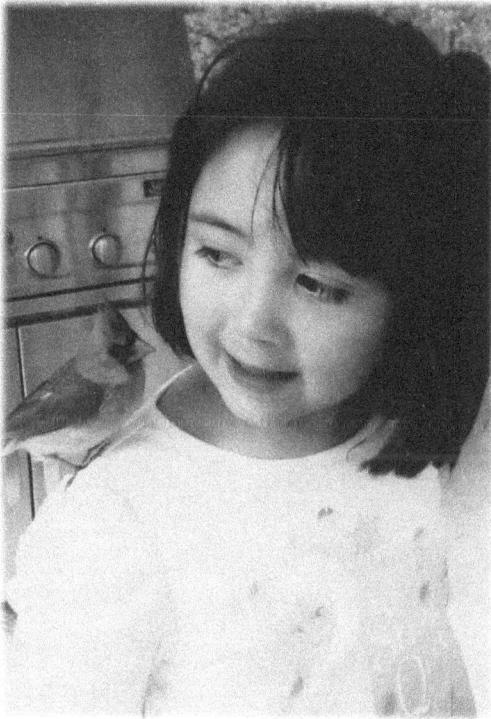

"I believe the female cardinal that landed on my granddaughter Anabelle's shoulder is Darlene in spirit, just letting us know she is still watching over her family."
–Allen Karl

www.ingramcontent.com/pod-product-compliance
Lightning Source LLC
Chambersburg PA
CBHW021951090426
42811CB00041B/2408/J